PASTORAL VISITATION

PASTORAL VISITATION

Nancy J. Gorsuch

FORTRESS PRESS   MINNEAPOLIS

PASTORAL VISITATION

Scripture quotations from the New Revised Standard Version of the Bible are copyright © 1989 by the Division of Christian Education of the National Council of Churches of Christ in the United States of America and are used by permission.

Cover design: Brad Norr
Cover photograph: Copyright © 1998 PhotoDisc, Inc.

Library of Congress Cataloging-in-Publication Data

Gorsuch, Nancy J.
     Pastoral visitation / Nancy J. Gorsuch.
          p.   cm. — (Creative pastoral care and counseling series)
     Includes bibliographical references.
     ISBN 0-8006-3190-0 (pbk. : alk. paper)
     1. Visitations (Church work)   I. Title.
BV4320.G67   1999
253'.7 — dc21   99-39380
                                                                            CIP

The paper used in this publication meets the minimum requirements of American National Standard for Information Sciences—Permanence of Paper for Printed Library Materials, ANSI Z329.48-1984.

Manufactured in the U.S.A.   AF 1-3190

03   02   01   00   99   1   2   3   4   5   6   7   8   9   10

Dedication

In memory of Barbara Gorsuch, my first caregiver

Acknowledgment

My sincere thanks to Howard Stone for the invitation
to write this book, and for his skillful guidance in its completion.

CONTENTS

EDITOR'S FOREWORD

Several years ago I visited with "Mike," a seminary student on a year-long internship. We were discussing life in the real world, his first full-time work in parish ministry. In the course of the conversation I asked him, "How do you find doing pastoral care in the parish?" His response: "I haven't done any. I'm in my office every morning and no one comes." At first I was taken aback, and then it dawned on me that he thought I was asking about pastoral counseling. I rephrased the question, asked him about the visitation of members in the hospital, in their homes, nursing homes, and the like. It turned out that Mike had done no pastoral visitation whatsoever in the first five months of his internship.

This pastoral intern was genuinely surprised that no one was calling on him for counseling. I felt less surprised several months later when I received a note from him telling me that he had been "pulled" from his internship and sent to another post. I never heard what events led to his reassignment, but I am certain that his failure to visit members of the congregation in their homes, or any other setting, was a contributing factor.

During the second half of the twentieth century, pastoral care ministry became dominated by pastoral counseling while to a great extent pastoral visitation is now considered anachronistic or unnecessary, perhaps even a nuisance, and often is simply jettisoned. What a loss! Church members lose the chance to sit down and talk with their pastors about their life of faith. Pastors lose the opportunity to get to know their parishioners intimately, and increasingly meet them only through worship or group meetings in the church.

Nancy Gorsuch is concerned about the erosion of pastoral visitation in pastoral ministry. In *Pastoral Visitation,* she demonstrates its critical role in the total ministry of the church. Her primary concern is not paying calls on church members in connection with crises, evangelism, or stewardship. Rather, it is personal contact for the care of the soul.

The first chapter of this book describes pastoral visitation and proposes reasons for its importance to parish ministry. This vital task not only helps pastors and church members to get better acquainted, but attends to parishoners' relationships with God and their discipleship as they follow Christ. The second chapter suggests several theological metaphors for visitation ministry. Here, Gorsuch helps the reader to consider the theological *why* of pastoral visitation. The third chapter is the *how*, offering specific ways in which caregivers can visit congregation members effectively. In it she suggests a collaborative approach to visitation—a partnership in the community of faith. She discusses the incorporation of worship, scripture, and prayer into pastoral visitation.

The fourth chapter points to the particular helping skills that pastoral caregivers use in their visitation ministry. Gorsuch focuses especially on listening and pastoral assessment. In addition, she addresses applicable issues of ethical conduct. The final chapter provides examples of several visitation programs used in churches and includes instructive details of how to initiate such programs. Gorsuch describes how the reader can move from intention to action and actually begin a visitation program or modify an existing one. She covers some administrative and organizational requirements, and enumerates specific guidelines for conducting pastoral visits. Finally, in the appendix she proposes a model for a training workshop for lay persons embarking on a visitation program.

One very helpful feature of the book is a "Steps to Action" section found at the end of each chapter. Here, Gorsuch helps readers move from theory to the actual implementation of an active visitation ministry in their parishes.

In our time, pastoral counseling, social action, marriage enrichment, and certainly preaching catch more attention than pastoral visitation; they are more glamorous, more visible. The significance of *Pastoral Visitation* is its thesis that visitation is nevertheless critical to our care of the soul, and indeed can help people become more faithful disciples. Readers are likely to be moved (as I was) by the thoughtful and creative way in which Nancy Gorsuch uncovers, illuminates, and elucidates this almost forgotten but richly rewarding task of ministry.

1

GOING TO SEE—
AN ACT OF MINISTRY

The elderly man sat in a chair by the window in his room, smiling as he spoke of his wife. "I miss her the most when I watch a baseball game. She loved baseball, you know . . . knew every player by name. Well, it's not the same anymore. Not that the people here aren't friendly. This is the right place for me so my son doesn't have to worry, but it does get lonesome sometimes without Betsy." The visitor from Al's congregation listened intently and hoped that his presence and the flowers he had brought from worship reminded Al of his friends in the congregation. "Sounds like you have good memories of those times with Betsy. I hear you still watch all the games and have tried to recruit your roommate as a fan. You always were good at getting others to join in and help out around the church. You know we miss you there and remember all that time and energy you gave."[1]

The mason jar had no handle and was too hot to pick up once the tea had been poured, and so the pastor waited. Maria continued talking as she prepared a cup for herself, apologizing that her dishes were all chipped or cracked except for the jar itself. A roach crawled along the flowers on the worn wallpaper above the stove behind her. She spoke of her dilemma with the landlord who had not completed the repairs to the apartment as she had requested, and asked if the pastor lived close to the church. They had met at the ecumenical agency when Maria had come for food assistance. During the interview for assistance, she had expressed interest in the single parent program sponsored by several area churches. The pastor had asked to come and visit her to talk more. Maria shared her concerns about the neighborhood school in which her two children were enrolled and described walking them to school each day to be sure they were safe. She was looking for a job so that she and the children could move to a better apartment in an adjoining neighborhood. "God has been so good to us," Maria said. "I know the Lord will continue to protect us."

They were seated at a table set with linen napkins and watched while the hostess filled the goblets with water and slices of fresh lemon. No printed menus were provided at the club and they listened as the waiter named the items being served for lunch that day. After placing their lunch orders, the pastor expressed appreciation for the opportunity to meet with Jim, one of the officers recently elected in the congregation. Jim had been a member of the congregation for many years and seemed a little hesitant when the pastor asked to visit him at his home. The pastor explained that visiting all the new officers was important in order to become better acquainted and to hear their hopes and concerns for the church's leadership in the coming year. "I think it would be more convenient if we meet for lunch at the club," Jim had said. "How about next Tuesday at noon?"

The Coke machine was located in the lobby of the inpatient facility, and they stopped for cans of soda before going out the door—pastor's treat. It was difficult to have a private conversation in the lounge with others present, so they agreed to take a walk outside and left word at the desk about where they would be. As they walked around the grounds of the rehabilitation center, the pastor asked Melissa how the first few days had gone for her. "It's been okay, I guess. It's better than going to jail." The pastor told Melissa that her parents had described some of what had happened and how she had agreed to the drug rehabilitation treatment as a first-time offender. "Your parents asked if I would come to see you," the pastor said. "But I didn't know whether you would want that or not. It's been a while since we've talked."

Pastoral visitation is an act of ministry in which a pastor or other caregiver goes to see a member or friend of a congregation. Like Jesus' encounter with Zaccheus, a caregiver may take the initiative and seek contact with a person in order to nurture a pastoral relationship. Telling someone we do not know well—"Hurry and come down—I must stay at your house today"—may sound intrusive to contemporary ears and is better posed as a request rather than a demand (Luke 19:5). But pastors and trained lay caregivers have a unique opportunity to visit others, to engage in pastoral conversation in a variety of settings, to nurture relationships of caring among members and friends of a congregation, and to enhance connections between the congregation and its wider community.

Pastoral calling and visitation often occur in response to particular needs, as an opportunity and privilege, to offer care and nurture in the personal context of someone's home (Jackson, 1990). Many obstacles exist in this aspect of caring ministry, including a caregiver's limited time and energy, which challenge motivation for sustaining initiative, especially for noncrisis visitation. The type of pastoral counseling used in a clinical setting has also contributed to an apparent shift to crisis-oriented or problem-focused understandings of pastoral conversation. Such counsel is crucial in pastoral ministry.

Some pastors have come to assume that people do not want to be visited because they are too busy. But current popular attention to spirituality of all sorts speaks of an abiding hunger for fuller relationship with God and for greater coherence in fragmented lives. I believe that pastoral visitation and the relationships it fosters can help to meet this longing. In what follows, I commend a reconsideration of noncrisis, nonproblem-focused pastoral visitation for purposes of extending care and nurture. Pastoral caregivers need to visit members and friends of the congregation to nurture them in faithfulness.

The comforting image of Jesus carrying a lamb in one arm, staff firmly in hand, has served as a primary metaphor for many caregivers. "The Lord is my shepherd," the psalmist says. The shepherd is the one who makes me lie down in green pastures, leads me beside still waters, restores my soul, leads me in right paths, prepares a table, anoints my head with oil (Ps. 23). "I am the good shepherd," Jesus claims in the gospel. "I know my own and my own know me, . . . and I lay down my life for the sheep" (John 10). Paul speaks to the elders, saying, "Keep watch over yourselves and over all the flock, of which the Holy Spirit has made you overseers, to shepherd the church of God" (Acts 20). The familiar biblical image of a comforting and guiding shepherd has shaped the identity of caregivers for ages and greatly influenced our theological reflection on acts of care. The shepherding image extends from Hebrew scriptures throughout the New Testament (examples include Jer. 3:15, Ezek. 34:23, John 10:2-14, John 24:15-17, and Acts 20:28). In large part, it is *this* understanding of God to which many caregivers witness in pastoral care, reflecting the divine shepherd of Hebrew faith and following the example of Jesus.

Shepherding was one of three "perspectives" in Seward Hiltner's pastoral theology, along with communicating and organizing, which signaled "a readiness, an attitude, or a point of view" that was never absent from the pastor/shepherd but not always the dominant perspective depending on the need being addressed (Hiltner, 1958). A pastor for whom the shepherding metaphor predominates would function as a guide, characterized by "care and solicitous concern" in Hiltner's terms. The image of a shepherd who guides still reflects the best of pastoral care, especially when the person of the shepherd balances courageous leadership with solicitous concern. The shepherd knows where the sheep need to go to meet their basic needs and is capable of showing them the way. The shepherd's responsibility for the flock is to offer protection, provision, and perhaps certain kinds of knowledge or competency.

At the risk of overworking the point, the following story provides some perspective on the relation between sheep and shepherd. Growing up on a farm in Iowa, I had the opportunity to feed my brother's sheep.

He maintained a small flock as part of a future farmers project, and occasionally it was my responsibility to take over his chores. I felt pretty sure of myself at the task as I dutifully carried two buckets of feed to the trough when, out of nowhere, a ram knocked me flat on my face. Still trying to figure out what had happened, I saw the ram backing up for another run, so I made a quick dash for the pickup truck. The sheep were left to fend for themselves that day from the feed spilled on the ground, and the shepherd, though not lost, was shaken up. Sheep are not helpless or undiscerning; they have their own integrity, power, and resourcefulness. Likewise, most parishioners do not like being pictured as sheep even if they find the image of the good shepherd quite comforting. Other metaphors for caregiving and discussion of power will be explored in the chapters to follow.

TAKING INITIATIVE

Al and his love of baseball, Maria pouring hot tea, Jim establishing the location for a visit, and Melissa walking the grounds of the rehabilitation center suggest the broad assortment of contexts and almost endless diversity of persons and situations of pastoral visitation. These care situations reflect in part the challenges caregivers face as they engage in this aspect of ministry. They reveal the types of visits in which care is offered and will serve as the basis for discussion of purpose and strategy in visitation.

Most pastors and lay leaders value visitation and make time to visit persons who have special needs, particularly in crisis situations. A number of valuable resources are available for pastoral response and intervention in times of crisis, but that is not the focus of this book (Stone, 1993; Switzer, 1989). Caregivers move from intention to action by broadening visits, seeking and nurturing relationships with persons who are not in crisis, and doing so because they value people and are interested in their lives of faith. Although capable pastors do well in responding to illness, grief, life transitions, family problems, and the range of identifiable needs in most congregations, *noncrisis visitation often falls by the way* as a lesser priority—important, but not important enough to make time, reserve emotional energy, and arrange in advance.

Pastors make several types of visits. They respond to crises, including predictable life events (illness and hospitalization, dying and death, bereavement, family problems). They visit those who are homebound or confined to a care center, and visit prospective members who have expressed interest through attending worship or inquiring about the congregation. They visit inactive members, members who are unhappy with the pastor or the church, make contacts for an annual stewardship fund-raising effort, and visit to recruit members for tasks and leadership needs of the church (Frank-Plumlee, 1988; Lyle, 1984; Shores, 1987).

In addition to these general types of visitation, I would add another— what could be called *ongoing every-member visitation* for the purpose of strengthening relationships with the caregiver, congregation, and community, and addressing issues of faith and its practice. This type of visitation may be accomplished during a visit for any of the reasons already discussed. But I am encouraging caregivers to think about every-member visitation as equally valuable and vital for persons of faith and the life of a faith community. Such visitation presumes that pastoral conversation has a special purpose and requires skills in listening, demonstrating regard for another's integrity and their sense of privacy about personal faith.

Every-member visitation presents an opportunity for dialogue about personal faith *and* its interpersonal and public expression in a specific cultural context—a conversation that is all too rare in a depersonalizing world. If caregivers assume that only more obvious needs require response, acts of pastoral care will be shaped entirely by the visible needs to which caregivers attend. They then miss the stories of faith finding expression through members' connections and commitments to their families or neighborhoods, where many times they are, without fanfare, acting in compassion and courage, with a sense of justice and hope. They also miss the tales of confusion or difficulty when efforts in faithful discipleship in a workplace or other group or institution have been frustrated or thwarted.

After Jesus told Zaccheus he was coming to his home that day, Zaccheus was happy, the gospel tells us, but others grumbled that Jesus was going to the house of a sinner. Zaccheus's response was to make restitution for his history of fraud, and in addition, he extended generosity to the poor. Jesus then declares, "Salvation has come to this house . . . for the Son of Man came to seek out and to save the lost" (Luke 19:6-10).

Pastoral visitation is not only ministry in response to need, but also "preventive" care, "calling forth" the work God is already accomplishing in a person's life. Visitation is "soul care," not private spirituality, but inquiring about a person's life in relation to God as a soul created in God's image and called to active, public discipleship. Discussing growth in faith and practice of discipleship happens in conversation with the caregiver or with someone else. The caregiver can nurture the life of the soul and its expression for those active members who were "found" by God long ago, as well as those who seem to be lost on their way.

The diversity and wonder of God's creation is manifest in the persons and situations caregivers encounter, which can be challenging and, in some moments, overwhelming. In some situations, a person's reaction can knock flat a caregiver. In others, the caregiver feels overwhelmed by the destructive forces of systemic sin intertwined in an individual's circumstance. The caregiver may be caught off guard by an angry response, misplaced or accurate, when constructive management of emotional intensity requires courage and skill. (Sometimes you just want to run for the truck.) A caregiver may become worn down and discouraged by cultural conditions of competition or violence that work against members' faithful efforts.

As persons of faith we trust that God is actively present in this amazing variety of humanity and in each individual's life, calling forth a particular response and leading that person forward. Perhaps the caregiver plays a crucial role as one who, for once, doesn't overreact to another's intense feelings. Across the gamut of situations caregivers encounter, we try to show the love and justice of God—as much as we are able to understand it —in our specific time and place. Further, as we visit in a residential care center, in a parishioner's home, across a table in a restaurant, or in a hospital or rehabilitation center, caregivers not only try to show the love and justice of God but to invite others to new or continued faithfulness. Encouraging persons in their practices of faith is a vital part of pastoral visitation, inviting conversation about discipleship, service to God and one's neighbors both within and beyond the congregation.

Many pastors and lay leaders encounter complaints from members of their congregation about the annual stewardship visit because it is sometimes the *only* time when organized visitation occurs. Visits initiated to fulfill the organizational needs of a local church have their place for stewardship and fund-raising, for evangelism and outreach, to contact inactive or prospective members, or to recruit leaders for particular tasks. But in addition to these legitimate and obvious needs, going to see a person may also be in response to needs that are not as apparent, which is the focus of pastoral visitation in this book. Pastoral caregivers often practice well-developed methods of regular visitation with members who are hospitalized or homebound, or who suffer from a chronic condition. Many congregations have a system of contacting persons who are experiencing grief to offer sustaining care either by phone or in person. These formal or informal networks of pastoral care are among the greatest strengths in many congregations, as all of us who have benefited from them in time of need know so well.

Face-to-face nurture of pastoral relationships for the sake of love and service may seem a puny goal compared to the list of objectives on most caregivers' to-do lists. However, the good intentions of caregivers are worth putting into action in an intentional—albeit nonheroic— process of pastoral visitation. Tending the members and friends of a community of faith may create a replenishing effect all around if the primary purpose is not (or not always) recruitment, problem solving, fund-raising, or any other valid purposes of visitation. Sometimes we need to visit folks because we're interested in them and their life of faith and discipleship more than the needs of the institution or organization we represent (Oates, 1982, 94).

PURPOSEFUL VISITATION

An intentional plan for visitation grows out of a clearly articulated purpose. It may feel like a waste of valuable time if a caregiver approaches every-member visitation with a goal of showing up at every parishioner's door. Pastors who are pressured to prove their value by reporting numbers of visits may slide into a superficial or even cynical approach to visiting in which everyone's expectations are so low that they will surely be met.

"High-commitment congregations" thrive. They are the churches in which members are expected to practice their faith in ministry and mission in a way that is often costly, even sacrificial, in personal time, energy, and resources. If the same is true for visitation by pastors and lay caregivers, raising expectations for accomplishments and stating this purpose clearly and publicly helps to sustain an effective program of visitation. Motivating caregivers to visit may not be the challenge, but rather developing strategy that sustains motivation and is workable in today's church (Frank-Plumlee, 1988, 61–62).

Visitation is a response to God's grace in which caregivers initiate pastoral conversation that addresses issues of faith and strengthens the web of interconnections among members, and between the congregation and its larger community. Such conversation may focus on a specific task in mission, or perhaps the person being visited volunteers at the local thrift shop, delivers Meals on Wheels, sends cards and engages in prayer for persons in special need, or plants flowers and pulls weeds in the memorial garden at the church. Pastoral conversation revolves around these acts of ministry as practices of faith and use of God-given gifts.

A caregiver visits and hears plans for marital separation or the cutoff in communication with a lifelong friend, and the possibility of reconciliation and forgiveness is discussed. A caregiver listens to the engineer who designs missile guidance systems for more accurate destruction, and they speak of contributing justice through a small but significant act of courage. A member tells a story about mediating racial conflicts within the local school board, and conversation takes shape around acting on convictions as an expression of faith. A caregiver hears the complaints of a member who has no time for prayer and meditation, and wonders with him about making space for spiritual replenishment in a too-busy life.

One of my favorite things about serving as a pastor in the local church was spending the morning working in my office and then doing something different in the afternoon—often some type of visitation. The combination of solitude and socializing, sitting still and moving about, fit well for me, and I enjoyed this built-in variety of pastoral ministry. I can easily recall the people I especially looked forward to visiting as a pastor because they took good care of me, affirmed my work, or showed exemplary courage in difficult circumstances, which heartened my own faith. I learned so much from their warm hospitality and generous spirits.

Pastoral visitation in response to special needs is part of what shapes most pastors' schedules. But a random approach to the every-member visitation recommended here cannot be sustained in the long run. It requires a strategy—a realistic strategy—if it is to be sustained. Several factors need to be considered in developing such a plan in a particular church or for the individual caregiver. Some factors to take into account include (a) congregational expectations regarding receiving visits and the pastor's use of time; (b) the pastor's ability and interest in visiting and availability; (c) staff or volunteer caregivers' availability if visitation is a shared ministry; (d) geographical proximity of locations for visits and ease of making contact—do members have phones?; and (e) shared understanding of the purpose of every-member visitation and its parameters (length, preferred location, whether a meal is expected, who the caregiver would like to have present).

Defining clearly what priority visitation will have for the pastor and other caregivers in the congregation, makes the planning much easier. The priority of visitation varies from church to church and can be established in a mutual process with a congregation's leaders. It can be identified through a pastor's position description or in setting goals and objectives for the church with lay leaders. Ecclesial style and understanding of authority—who decides how pastors use their time—also varies widely among congregations and denominations. Some congregations expect that every family should receive one visit in their home per year from the pastor. Other congregations communicate a sense that they are too busy for their pastor to visit or that they want the pastor's time used in response to more critical needs.

A well-publicized and shared understanding of the priority and purpose of every-member visits is a key point in developing intentional, planned visitation. The pastor or caregiver's availability affects visitation strategy, and the willingness to do some visits on evenings and weekends is necessary in most churches. Many pastors find that planning two visits per week for pastoral conversation (in addition to the crisis, hospital, care center visits that are a part of the pastor's routine) is a realistic goal. Of course, much more becomes possible if a group of lay caregivers are available and prepared to participate in every-member visits. Coordinating the efforts of such a group means good communication with the pastor, planning how many members each caregiver will visit over a stated period of time, and perhaps some "matching" of caregiver with parishioner on the basis of proximity or some other criterion.

If lay caregivers are recruited and trained for every-member visitation and the purpose is for pastoral conversation, then an instrument such as a "questionnaire" or "inventory" as a basis for conversation guides the caregivers and provides more continuity among those conversations. (Suggestions for such an instrument will be offered in chapter 3.) Visitation may be part of a larger church program that encourages commitment to particular forms of ministry or mission by each member based on a time and talents survey. Viewing any visitation strategy as an experiment for a few weeks or months and setting a specific time to evaluate what is working well and what needs to be changed creates opportunities for evaluation and adjustment.

CONSIDERING CONTEXT

When the visitor from the church sat with Al at the care center, he was privileged to hear Al's cherished memories and to recollect Al's participation in their community of faith. This caregiver was engaged in an act of ministry on behalf of the congregation, listening to feelings of grief and loneliness, honoring this man's contributions to his church, and helping him to sense that he is still connected to and part of the life of that congregation.

When the pastor visited Maria in her home, she listened to Maria's concerns for herself and her children, her hopes about employment and moving to better housing, her faith in God's providence. The pastor actively witnessed Maria's faith in God and her courage to persevere in the midst of difficult circumstances. The visit was at the pastor's initiative, inviting Maria to participate in a church program, but resulted from contact at a larger ecumenical program in which area churches reach out to the neediest in their community.

When the pastor had lunch with Jim at the club in order to become better acquainted with his hopes as an officer of the church, Jim identified the location he preferred for a visit. The visit was a little like a "business" lunch at which Jim was in charge, but they did become better acquainted. The conversation opened the opportunity for inquiring about his commitment to the congregation and beginning to hear the story of this member's personal faith, struggles, and growth.

When the pastor went to the residential treatment center to visit Melissa, it was not at her request. The terms of the visit needed to be negotiated with Melissa herself, fulfilling her parents' request but also having regard for Melissa's feelings and not intruding on her privacy. Going to see this young woman and engaging her in conversation about her difficulties also created the space for hearing some of her hopes and dreams, which were not reflected in the harmful choices she had made. A caregiver has the chance to invite other healthier, hopeful parts of Melissa's story into a pastoral conversation and to expand on these alternative parts of her journey.

Initially, none of these visits appear to lead toward the type of pastoral conversation I have described. Pastoral visitation lends itself to a kind of *leadership that values inquiring about a person's life of faith,* doing so in a nonintrusive way (see chapter 3). This personal kind of conversation calls for interpersonal skills and active listening. At the same time, privatism is a cultural force that intersects with faith often to the detriment of practicing faith. Pastoral theologian Larry Graham states that caretaking in the face of current cultural forces involves evaluating patterns of living and the quality of life they make possible.

> A culturally sensitive ministry of care recognizes that persons are adrift, without moorings, and that the communities which nurtured their visions of reality often no longer sustain or support them. It is sensitive to the conflicting pulls upon individuals and communities from a radically pluralistic world order. It seeks to reconnect persons and communities with their traditions, while at the same time assisting with the construction of new traditions that are responsive to the personal needs and historical realities of our time. (Graham, 1992, 59)

Historicism, one of three cultural forces Graham names, means that caregivers need some perspective on current patterns of living that are supported by the culture, especially any dehumanizing or depersonalizing patterns. The force or influence of culture may be seen as people live out patterns of behavior that conform to the norm or standard of a culture even if the behavior is at odds with other values they hold. Caregivers can identify patterns of living peculiar to a particular culture and a specific period in time and, in the very act of visiting, provide an alternative.

Depersonalizing, dehumanizing patterns of living often reduce inter-action to an exchange of goods and information. Caregivers who take the time for noncrisis, face-to-face visits, resist these cultural forces. Visita-tion for the purpose of nurturing relationship and fostering faithfulness is, in my opinion, one of the most caring acts of contemporary pastoral ministry. Caregivers hear others' longing for a sense of well-being in the midst of multiple, fragmenting commitments, help to identify their personal choices that maintain the problem (and conform to cultural standards), and look at possible other choices (as practice of faithful-ness to God and neighbor). Caretaking involves providing alternatives to a culture in which material forces contend for power and influence, most notably the violence that results from an unjust distribution of material resources (Graham, 1992, 60). Graham points out a third cul-tural factor at work: along with historicism and materialism is pri-vatism, which focuses interest on intrapsychic and interpersonal dynamics as separate from the larger, public social order (1992, 60). A congregation's program of pastoral visitation engages individuals in conversation to attend to their inner and interpersonal life, and explores the impact of cultural forces that may generate and perpetuate prob-lems in the individual and family's life, in the congregation itself, and in the community in which it is located. Pastoral visitation in the current cultural milieu means *attending to and nurturing a personal life of faith, and inviting and encouraging public expression of that faith—what I call fostering faithfulness.*

The discussion of visitation as a response to crisis or special needs can be found in a number of works that address pastoral care more generally (Clinebell, 1984; Coyle, 1985; Frank-Plumlee, 1988; Hiltner, 1958, 1959; Holifield, 1983; Lyle, 1984; Krass, 1987; Oates, 1982; Oden, 1983; Shores, 1987; Stone and Clements, 1991). This book however seeks to encourage pastoral visits with a broader purpose. Throughout this project, I draw upon a number of resources specific to my own denomination. I recall a local clergy luncheon I attended twenty years ago when a pastor gave the blessing before the meal, another least-common-denominator prayer out of respect for the diversity of people present. One of the rabbis said something like, "I'd really prefer if you would go ahead and use the name of Jesus Christ; otherwise, I'm not sure what you're talking about." I am using denominational sources from a particular branch of a faith tradition, so that readers know more of what I'm talking about.

The following chapter offers an invitation to consider a theology of visitation based upon purposes for visitation "inherited" from the Christian tradition and current issues in pastoral theology. Chapter 3 explores the spiritual and ritual leadership of the caregiver through pastoral conversation, and suggests a guided reflection on faithfulness as a basis for such conversation. Chapter 4 focuses on equipping caregivers with interpersonal listening skills as a means of care and nurture, and briefly discusses issues of power and authority, confidentiality, and ethical conduct in this aspect of care. Chapter 5 includes several illustrations of congregational programs that connect individuals, congregations, and community; the steps in formulating a visitation program; and guidelines for a particular visit. The appendix offers an outline for a visitation training workshop.

Steps to Action

1. Identify the type and frequency of visits that already occur in your congregation and note any feedback you have received.

2. In a sentence or two, write down the purpose of visitation in your church as it currently exists.

3. List the aspects of the environment in which visits occur in your ministry setting that, if considered more fully, might influence the purpose, types and frequency of visits made.

4. Name two steps you will take in the next week that will continue a process of change in your approach to pastoral visitation (conversation with colleagues about visitation in their congregations, further reading on the subject, asking for feedback from two church leaders about current visitation).

2

FOSTERING FAITHFULNESS—
A THEOLOGY OF VISITATION

Going to see the family of confirmation class members was part of nurturing their growth in faith and its practice. When the pastor, Ron, went to Jerry's home it was the first time he'd met Jerry's father, Mr. Greene. Mrs. Greene sang in the choir and though she was quiet, the pastor thought she was pleased and proud that Jerry was making a commitment to membership. As Ron sat down in their living room, Mr. Greene greeted him from across the room without getting up, and continued watching TV and drinking from a six-pack of beer beside his chair. After a failed attempt at including Jerry's father in conversation, the pastor continued talking with Mrs. Greene and Jerry. Then, somewhat exasperated, he turned to Mr. Greene and said, "Would you please turn the TV off so we could talk for a few minutes? I made an effort to get here at a time you would be home so that I could at least meet you. I want to make sure you're going to be at worship on Sunday because it means a lot to your son, and you should be there. Can I count on you?"

Carmen was a lay caregiver who had found her niche visiting members of the congregation who resided in a local care center. Though new to the pastoral care committee at her church, she knew her extrovert personality was a big plus when it came to visiting. The pastor, who was headed out of town for vacation, had asked Carmen to visit an older couple from the congregation sometime in the next week. Though they still lived in their own home, the woman had recently undergone a mastectomy and was receiving chemotherapy. The prognosis was not good. Carmen had made the visit, but felt anxious about what she'd said—or hadn't said—when the older woman spoke of not wanting to continue treatment. Carmen had offered what she hoped were encouraging words of comfort, but afterwards she felt unsettled about the encounter, as if she'd been cheerful, but not helpful. Carmen spoke about this experience with the committee of lay caregivers, who met once a month for peer support and information sharing. She wondered about finding a book she could read or something that would help the whole group understand more about dying and how we should talk about it as Christians.

Noel was riding the bus to his class at the community college when he saw that the woman seated across the aisle from him was crying. He'd seen her before on this same route and assumed she was on her way home from work. He hesitated, not wanting to intrude on her privacy, but he was concerned about her apparent distress. He decided to risk it, pulled a pack of Kleenex from his pocket, and handed them across to her. She was startled, but thanked him, and after blowing her nose, said "I'm just having a really bad day . . . a lot of bad days. I don't know what I'm going to do. Can't pay my rent. Can't keep food on the table. Nobody gives a damn whether I live or die anymore. It's just too much. Too much." Noel said, "I'm sorry you're having such a hard time. Is there anybody who can help you, a friend or relative or something?" "Nobody," she said. "Ain't nobody cares about me anymore. But I've gotten by before, and I'll get by again. You've been nice to me, though, and I thank you." The bus pulled up to Noel's stop. He stood up to leave and said, "I wish I could help. Please take care. Maybe I'll see you again Thursday—same time, same seat?" The woman chuckled and smiled at him, "Well, Kleenex is what I needed today. Kleenex is what I got! See you Thursday, maybe."

Why should we visit the Greenes or the older couple, or speak with the tearful woman on the bus? Does our faith require it? Is it a ministry of the church? This chapter invites consideration of a theological rationale for visitation. The three brief vignettes portray some strengths and some limitations in pastoral caregivers responding to particular needs. Several issues are raised by what did and didn't happen in these vignettes: What makes a visit or conversation "pastoral"? How does a caregiver balance more receptive hearing and more active assertion in leading a pastoral conversation? What skills help a caregiver to structure and shape such encounters? What preparation is needed for a particular visit? What does such interaction have to do with a congregation, a local community, or wider cultural influences at work?

Jesus says of the righteous, "I was hungry and you gave me food, I was thirsty and you gave me something to drink, I was a stranger and you welcomed me, I was naked and you gave me clothing, I was sick and you took care of me, I was in prison and you visited me" (Matt. 25:35-36). For ministers of care, going to see someone in the hospital or at home may seem such a routine act of pastoral ministry that it hardly requires thoughtful theological reflection. A caregiver may claim "but I'm not a theologian!" and assume that when equipped with sufficient helping skills, knowledge of the Bible will be an adequate basis for visitation. Scripture is an excellent place to begin and to return again and again (Capps, 1981; Oglesby, 1980; Oates, 1982; Oden, 1983). My own understanding and use of scripture is, of course, shaped by the faith tradition in which I was nurtured, in which a variety of views on this subject coexist.[2]

The theology implicit in our acts of care is probably more powerful than our explicitly held theology. Consider the following clusters of questions, which may expose theological assumptions significant for pastoral care, and open the opportunity for critical and constructive reflection.[3]

1. How do you understand God, God's relationship to creation, and how God is involved with us and our world? Is it the Creator's fixed plan that we receive and follow, or are we free to do whatever we choose and bear the consequences, or somewhere in between?

2. What is your theological view of humanity? Are we fundamentally flawed or basically good, primarily social or existentially isolated, created in the image of God as a glimmer or a fuller reflection? Does sin have to do with pride or passivity, triumphalism or hopelessness, misuse of freedom or not enough freedom, trying to be God or refusing God's image in us? Is sin something "in" individuals or is it "in" groups, institutions, and culture in more systemic form?

3. What do you think is our purpose as human beings, and more specifically, as the church in the midst of creation? Is it to glorify God and to enjoy God forever as the Westminster Shorter Catechism says? Is it to reach our full human potential; to do justice, show mercy, and walk humbly with God; to increase love of God, neighbor, and self? How do you view the church, as the people in covenant relation with God, or as the body of Christ living in and for the world, or as a community of the Spirit? Do we offer pastoral care only within the church or does it extend beyond the faith community?

4. What is the relation between salvation or redemption, and health, wholeness, and growth? Do caregivers issue a call to faith, emphasizing conversion, or an invitation to discipleship and practicing faith as God's grace is appropriated? Are we promoting health—physical, emotional, and spiritual well-being—and, if so, how do we define a "healthy" person? Are we addressing instances where sin, evil, or injustice is at work in both personal and systemic forms, and so identifying distortions of freedom and promoting justice and equity through social change? If our caring assumes God is the one who redeems, makes justice, ends suffering, brings the new creation, how do caregivers participate in what God is already doing?

We do not have to have the answers to all these theological issues, but pastoral caregivers need to be familiar with the questions and aware of their operative assumptions because they dramatically influence the care we offer.[4] A caregiver makes choices in any act of interpersonal ministry, which implies answers to these questions, theology implicated in what is said and not said, the language and terms used, and the values and attitudes embedded in the caring process. Many pastoral caregivers attend first to clarifying their theological anthropology, suggested in the second cluster of questions. Some begin with reassessing their understanding of who God is and how God is revealed in the coming of Jesus Christ, through scripture, the Christian community, and the wider history of God's grace at work in the world.

METAPHORS FOR CAREGIVING

Pastor Ron's encounter with the Greene family ended on a rather sour note when he left their home, and he felt disappointed about his effort to get Mr. Greene to come to worship. On the following Sunday morning, Mrs. Greene came to his study before worship with her choir robe on and music folder in hand. She said, "I'm sorry my husband wasn't very nice to you. He gets in these moods, especially when he's had a few beers, and so we don't have people over much. I still don't know whether he's coming to church today." The pastor replied, "Well, that's all right. I came on pretty strong with him. Sounds like he drinks quite a bit. Is this a problem for him, or for you, if you don't mind my asking?" From there, the pastor took the conversation in the direction of a referral for the Greenes to receive counseling, and consultation about what could be done to address Mr. Greene's problematic use of alcohol and its consequences for their family. He continued to "check in" with Mrs. Greene and with Jerry on a regular basis to see how things were going.

Pastor Ron's visit was an intentional part of his care for confirmands and their families. He overreacted a bit to Mr. Greene's unexpected behavior and moved a little toward "bullying," a distortion of the shepherd image encountering a situation beyond his control. But he did firmly express his purpose for visiting, gathered information that was very helpful to Mrs. Greene, and followed through on his commitment to continuing care for these family members to the extent they would allow it. As an illustration of the shepherding metaphor, Pastor Ron's competence and responsible leadership are among the things his congregation appreciates. He is not easily daunted by difficult situations and communicates directly, sometimes a little too directly, what he thinks and what he would like to have happen. A little more "tender and solicitous concern" and more empathic responses would strengthen his pastoral care, but nonetheless his actions speak on behalf of effectiveness in garnering resources when needed.

Biblical metaphors evoke ancient biblical images, suggest interpersonal dynamics, and specify particular understandings of who God is and how we are to respond to God's grace (McFague, 1982). Metaphors for caregiving powerfully shape pastoral identity and have been explored by a number of pastoral theologians, notably Alastair Campbell (1981) and Donald Capps (1981; 1984). Alastair Campbell has encouraged caregivers to reclaim their theological imagination, suggesting that when "operating metaphors" become limited, our care does also. In an effort to recover the integrity of pastoral care by restoring biblical images, he explored the courageous leadership of the shepherd, the healing power of "wounded love," and the prophetic wisdom of the fool, as they are found in scripture.

For most pastoral caregivers, one of these biblical metaphors for caregiving resonates well with one's self-understanding. Of course, as Campbell points out, it is best if we can demonstrate some or all of these metaphors in our ministry. The three metaphors for caregiving suggest pastoral self-understandings, which inform a pastor's praxis or interpretation of and approach to a problem.[5]

Courageous leadership is the primary characteristic of the most familiar biblical metaphor for caregiving (Campbell, 1981). "With upright heart he tended them, and guided them with skillful hand" (Ps. 78:72). The shepherd of the Bible demonstrates courage in words, actions, and of course in suffering and self-sacrifice. The shepherd was the dominant model for caregiving in the 1960s and 1970s, popularized in the work of Seward Hiltner as a perspective or attitude in ministry of "tender and solicitous concern" (1958, 1959). The strengths of this ancient metaphor are the combination of courage and tenderness invoked, suggesting skillful mobilizing of resources and solicitous concern in a capacity to suffer on behalf of another.

Pastoral care based on a shepherding metaphor would demonstrate competent leadership, exercise skill in helping, take responsibility for the care of others, encourage freedom but within boundaries, and protect against destructive forces beyond safe territory. The shepherd knows the sheep, the territory, the dangers, and where the oases are, and uses a firm and gentle hand in guiding the flock. The understanding of God implied in the metaphor is that God can be trusted and hope justified. Carried too far, a kind of triumphal theology can enter in with a caregiver plunging in to fix most anything. The drawbacks or potential distortions in caregiving based on this metaphor may be taking too much responsibility for another, denying their agency and freedom, offering advice as a kind of expert, or even outright bullying if a sense of aggressive superiority has overtaken the biblical portrayal.

The second metaphor from scripture was popularized in the 1970s in Henri Nouwen's work of the same name, and the notion of the suffering God was explored systematically in Moltmann's theology (Nouwen 1972;

Moltmann 1974). The wounded healer, as Campbell notes, is central to the Christian understanding of Jesus' death. Certainly the image of Jesus in Gethsemane before his betrayal informs this metaphor. When he became distressed he said to the disciples, "I am deeply grieved, even to death; remain here and stay awake with me" (Matt. 26:37), and his words of suffering on the cross, "My God, my God, why have you forsaken me?" (Matt. 26:46).

The wounded healer metaphor is not only about suffering, but about wounding that is healed, reconciled, mending what was broken. "Do not be afraid; I know that you are looking for Jesus who was crucified. He is not here; for he has been raised, as he said" (Matt. 28:5-6). Paul understood God's consolation in his suffering as enabling him to console others. "For just as the sufferings of Christ are abundant for us, so also our consolation is abundant through Christ. If we are being afflicted, it is for your consolation and salvation; if we are being consoled, it is for your consolation which you experience when you patiently endure the same sufferings that we are also suffering" (2 Cor. 1:5-6).

As a metaphor for caregiving, one's own experiences of wounding in grief and loss, and personal experiences of healing or moving through the pain, create a space for resonance with another's pain. As much by presence as by words, this approach in pastoral care conveys an awareness and a transcendence of loss. The "healing power of wounded love" is expressed in openness to self-examination and the ability to identify feelings, using one's inner life as a resource for emotional availability to others (as opposed to the shepherd who looks around for resources). Prayer, meditation, and self-reflection are particularly necessary in this model for pastoral care. Sharing one's feelings, encouraging deeper relationship with the other person, engaging in a ministry of presence and vulnerability all characterize this metaphorical approach to care.

The understanding of God implied in this metaphor emphasizes God's pathos, the one who suffers with us and cares deeply about our pain. Some caregivers prefer to focus on Jesus as comforting friend or companion in this approach, but one drawback is that a sense of God's sovereignty, power, and work in the world is often needed. The hazards in using this image of pastoral care may limit one's purpose to eliciting insight at an emotional level without acting upon it, a type of passivity that underemphasizes an individual's agency and overuses empathic or solicitous responses so that personal and social change do not occur. Burn out, emotional or spiritual desolation, and depression are all potential issues for caregivers working from this self-understanding. Less experienced caregivers may forget the "healer" part of their self-identification or lack clarity in boundaries between self and other.

The third metaphor is probably the least known of the three, but an intriguing addition to awareness of biblical images for care. The metaphor is based on the "reversal" of wisdom in scripture: "For God's foolishness is wiser than human wisdom, and God's weakness is stronger than human strength" (1 Cor. 1:25); "Do not deceive yourselves. If you think that you are wise in this age, you should become fools so that you may become wise. For the wisdom of this world is foolishness with God" (1 Cor. 3:18-19); "Therefore I am content with weaknesses, insults, hardships, persecutions, and calamities for the sake of Christ; for whenever I am weak, then I am strong" (2 Cor. 12:10).

The wise fool image appeared in a work by Faber depicting ministers in a hospital setting as similar to a clown in a circus, relieving anxiety and looking like an amateur among skilled tight rope walkers (1971). In contrast to an ordered, "professional" world, the wise fool is loyal not to norms, conventions, or authorities in society, but to alternative perspectives and informality. Appearing a bit naive, unsophisticated, and sometimes irreverent, the wise fool knows how to laugh. The metaphor is similar to images in literature of the court jester who guides indirectly and feigns stupidity so that the king will think the solution was his own bright idea.

The prophetic quality of the fool's wisdom is the distinguishing feature of this metaphor. Micah's pointed statement of our purpose exemplifies the wise fool's approach: "And what does the Lord require of you but to do justice, and to love kindness, and to walk humbly with your God?" (Micah 6:8). Loyalty is another characteristic, steadfastness even when others may have given up on a person or a purpose. The pastoral care offered by someone from this perspective would be marked by simplicity and alternative images of power and prosperity, a loyal kind of love that remains steadfast, humor that enhances flexibility and endurance. A wise fool would likely challenge distortions in what is being said, trusting that if a problem is understood more "truthfully" from an alternate view, the resolution will become clear.

Care based on this metaphor helps people alter their view of themselves and their problems (as opposed to the wounded healer who looks to inner resources or the shepherd who looks around for resources). The wise fool may call the church to accountability for its practice of faith, and engage in social action. The understanding of God suggested in this metaphor is a call for truth rather than self-deception, for practicing what we say we believe. Liabilities of the metaphor for purposes of caregiving are that foolishness without wisdom can devolve into incompetence and spontaneity, which indicates an irresponsible lack of preparation. Though a "not-knowing" position may be a useful antidote to a condescending assumption of expertise, it can be carried too far when firmer guidance is needed.

This review of three biblical metaphors for caregiving has explored the strengths and drawbacks of each image, and suggested an understanding of God implied in each. It is not intended to be comprehensive or conclusive, but to stir the imagination of what theological assumptions a caregiver brings to any act of ministry such as visitation, and to expose assumptions for more critical and constructive reflection.

INTEGRITY AND PLURALISM

Carmen's experience in offering care to the woman who was seriously ill became part of her learning experience. Through this learning process over the next year, Carmen became a caregiver who reflected many of the strengths of the wounded healer, but it took time. As a result of talking about her visit with the other pastoral care committee members, she discovered that grief was an issue for many members of the church, particularly with recent deaths of two beloved longtime members. The committee worked with the pastors to plan and implement a six-month focus on faith and meaning in the midst of dying and death. The committee members received further training in supportive visitation with persons experiencing loss and grief. They visited a funeral home to understand some of the decisions a family faces when a loved one dies, and identified several ways they could be of help. They became interested in encouraging members to preplan their own funeral or memorial services, gathered and distributed information on ethical choices in prolonging or ending life, and on advanced care directives. This wider church program included a series of sermons during Lent addressing biblical and theological views of dying, death, and what it means to be "resurrection people" who have "Easter faith," but who do not contradict the pain of loss with too-triumphal proclamation. The education committee hosted a series of small group discussions based on a film series addressing different types of loss. What began as a visit by a rather tentative wounded-not-sufficiently-healed caregiver, flourished in a congregation capable of using its organizational structure in response to a pastoral care need. It occurred to Carmen during the committee's training process, that one reason she stayed cheerful during that early visit, rather than more accurately reflecting the concerns of the woman who was ill, was her own difficulty with lingering grief. A process of prayer, meditation, and pastoral conversation for her own needs, and the "work of the Spirit" to use her words, provided powerful healing.

Noel's simple act of kindness was a small risk, going against the "never talk to strangers" rule-of-thumb. Although they didn't ever know one another well, Noel spoke with the woman each time they were on the bus together that semester, and she began to ask about his classes and his plans for the future. Sometimes he'd pull a Kleenex packet from his pocket to show her, and she'd laugh and say, "No, thank you, it didn't get that bad today!" He remembered this experience partly because he felt as though he hadn't done anything, but it felt good, whatever "it" was.

A city bus is an unusual place for a pastoral visit, but then why not take the opportunity when and where it presents itself? Elements of the wise fool metaphor are evident in Noel's humor and humility, in part, because it was outside the bounds of "official" ministry of the church and because the woman was not seeking pastoral care per se. It is "pastoral" care not by association with an ordained office in the church, but to the extent that it is an extension of the ministry of Jesus Christ, a ministry in which all believers are called to engage. Noel himself didn't think about it that way at first, but this story of care, when it is told and interpreted as such, illustrates simple foolish wisdom. More important, it is the kind of story that continues to influence Noel himself and the woman on the bus. Who knows how far a little leaven can go?

Theological Implications

A number of issues have begun to emerge in the biblical metaphors for caregiving, each of which has implications for a theology of visitation. First, integration of the strengths in each metaphor and attention to the potential distortions require a type of tender and firm leadership, personal awareness and interpersonal skills, and prophetic imagination. Pastoral visitation involves leadership based upon worship as the forming center of Christian community, discerning the potential role of proclamation and teaching in pastoral conversation.

However, a second issue in a theology of visitation concerns the nature of Christian community as it is shaped in a local congregation. Pastoral theologian Charles Gerkin has described the need for a shift in local congregations from being a "centripetal," or "pastor-centered" community, oriented through gathering of community, toward a more "centrifugal," outward focused congregation oriented as the people of God "disbursed" into a variety of community relationships (1991, 116–42).

In contrast to the confining, enclosing imagery of the centripetal model, this schematization of the centrifugal model of the Christian community envisions that community as primarily involved in preserving and nourishing a body of meanings and style of relationship by which all other communal relationships are to be understood, fostered, and evaluated. [These meanings] are to be disbursed into all other levels and varieties of community relationships, rather than to be treasured and harbored within the Christian community itself. (Gerkin, 1991, 137)

The differences between centripetal and centrifugal understandings of Christian community may dramatically influence the authority attributed to a caregiver, the purpose of visitation, and the content of pastoral conversation if it is to focus on faithfulness.

A third issue to be considered in a theology of visitation is equipping persons to offer care, utilizing knowledge from supporting disciplines (such as psychotherapy) while maintaining pastoral identity and integrity, shaped by a particular congregation's identity and understanding of community. Assessment that takes into account the social and cultural influences upon persons we encounter in visitation broadens the scope of what caregivers inquire about, and the responses they are equipped to offer. Offering care through ethical conduct and appropriate personal boundaries, with adequate preparation and follow-up, using consultation before reaching the limits of one's competence all involve a caregiver's self-awareness and regard for difference.

Fourth, the notion of prophetic pastoral care affirms a link between a particular ministry setting and the faith tradition in which it occurs, identifying the place of social action and advocacy in relation to visitation.[6] Forming a community of faith in the context of a larger community means identifying the congregation's strengths and points of linkage or connection with needs in the community, with an attitude of disbursement in and collaboration with efforts in the wider community, not just institutional maintenance. At first, it may seem to be an issue of outreach ministry or local mission rather than pastoral care. But attention to context, the relationship between the congregation and its local community, dramatically influences what happens or doesn't happen in a program of visitation.

REFLECTION ON ACTION

Thinking through what has happened during a pastoral visit makes it more likely that the purpose of visitation will be fulfilled in future visits. Ongoing reflection on acts of ministry is most helpful in a consultative relationship or caregivers group (with the congregation's knowledge), opening acts of ministry to dialogue and broadened understanding so that caregiving responses emerge from both faith commitments and good information. Such consultation also helps caregivers to recognize needs for ongoing training, to celebrate their own growth in faith and its practice, and to care for themselves properly while they attend to others. We may assume that what we believe about God, humanity, and the divine-human relationship is accurately reflected in acts of ministry based upon the image of Jesus as shepherd. We may trust that fostering faith and guiding the life and mission of a particular community occur without much critical thinking in the acts of care we offer. And it is true that a kind of "operative" theology based on our beliefs is demonstrated in visitation whether or not we reflect critically and constructively on the biblical and theological basis for visitation. Theological reflection on practice of ministry leads to greater congruence between what one believes, what one knows and learns, and what one does with it in caring for another (though I have heard some say demonstrating their confusion is exactly what they fear most).[7]

The traditional sources for theological reflection—scripture, tradition, experience, and reason—come fully into play in assessing a theological rationale for visiting. A theology of visitation emerges from reflection on biblical images of care, needs encountered and purposes served in visitation, and experience in visiting, both personal experience and that reflected in pastoral care literature.

Several sources of knowledge need to be considered for reflection in pastoral theology, understood as a branch of the wider theological tradition (Graham, 1992, 20–23). Larry Graham discusses sources that include a specific practice of ministry, the social and cultural context of that ministry, the living religious tradition, a cognate secular discipline (such as psychology or sociology), and the social location and personhood of the caregiver (sex, age, race, sexual orientation, economic status, and the like). The shape of pastoral ministry is heavily influenced not only by the biblical tradition it reflects, but by the social and cultural forces at work, and the particular stream of faith tradition with its own convictions about God, humanity, our purpose, and the meaning of salvation and well-being that we promote.

In addition, supporting disciplines—often psychology or psychotherapy—and a critical social/political perspective, such as feminist theory, help to expose the limitations of assumptions and inform our ministry. Certainly the social location and personhood of the caregiver—gifts and graces, personal limits and persistent wounds—all are sources for reflection in discerning one's theological basis for visitation. I offer the following reflections on these sources of knowledge for a pastoral theology of visitation as an example.

Offering pastoral care has been a part of my pastoral ministry through fifteen years of service in a variety of local congregations, some of which is reflected in the illustrations included in this book. Practice of ministry and focus on specific situations of pastoral care form a primary basis for reflection among caregivers as we evaluate and enhance the care we offer. The social and cultural setting for a specific instance of pastoral care can be more fully discerned by using a critical social or political theory that exposes the limits of the caregiver's perspective and the forces potentially at work. For instance, identifying the effects of historicism, materialism, and privatism embedded in a specific situation enables caregivers to perceive forces that precipitate or perpetuate problems. Alternative patterns or additional options for consideration then become more clear. In my pastoral ministry, I have used feminist theory, both theological and therapeutic, to help analyze differences in power and assumptions about roles of women, which may be causing or at least contributing to difficulties (Couture, 1991; Miller-McLemore, 1994; Neuger, 1996; Poling, 1991; Russell, 1979, 1987).

The living religious tradition in which I work is the Presbyterian branch of the Reformed tradition.[8] As noted earlier, my personal history is shaped through nurturing in this faith perspective and by the dilemmas of ongoing interpretation, revisioning, and reforming, which are a part of this tradition. The cognate or "supporting disciplines" of psychology and psychotherapy, which informed my pastoral ministry for years, were influenced by interest in depth psychology and humanistic psychology, particularly the work of Carl Rogers (1961). Currently, I am influenced by works in feminist psychotherapy, solution-focused approaches, and narrative therapeutic theory.[9] The caregiving I offer is shaped through my social location as a white woman, marriage partner and mother, middle-aged, middle-class, ordained Presbyterian and seminary teacher.

These sources of knowledge influence and inform the caregiving I offer, and the clearer I become in recognizing the relative influence of each source, the more I am able to critically and constructively reflect on and enhance effectiveness in pastoral ministry. Self-identification along these lines is a necessary starting point for caregivers so that we do not assume we have an "objective" view of any situation we encounter, but are able to "own" and assess the limits of our knowledge and, in some cases, actively compensate for those limits.

A pastoral theology of visitation based on the sources I have identified in my own work as pastoral theologian carries many implications. Other caregivers will identify alternative sources that inform their theology of visitation in different ways that are more appropriate to their practice of ministry, social and cultural environment, religious tradition, preferred supporting discipline, and social location as caregiver. Fostering faithfulness is one way of naming a theological perspective on pastoral visitation that fits well with my own sources of knowledge and experience base. The Reformed tradition affirms the priority of God's grace to which we respond in faith. This emphasis on God's grace and initiative is a specific understanding of the nature of God, which leads to emphasis on faithfulness as our purpose in response to God's grace. Fostering faithfulness does not mean that caregivers bring about such a response by promoting a kind of "works righteousness" for caregivers or those who seek care. Fostering faithfulness does not imply that we can attain a state or condition of grace if only we try hard enough (Presbyterian Church, 1989, 1990).

Coming to faith and growing in the life of faith rely upon the prior activity of God as the source of faith, and view faith as response to God's initiative in covenant and incarnation. Growing in faith or being on a journey as disciples are popular biblical images that help us think about our responses to God. But an emphasis on "progress" in faithfulness, an organic kind of "natural" growth process, or stages of development and maturing in the life of faith may miss three key points. First, fostering faithfulness and practicing faith involve not only human capacities and interactions, but also alignment with and participation in the work of God's grace in the world, inasmuch as we are able to understand it. Second, the nurture of faith and its practices is a communal experience.

"New life in Christ" is made available to us in community. Such community carries on its life through certain "practices" that are constitutive of the shape of its life together in the world. These practices were called by Calvin "external means or aims by which God invites us into the society of Christ and holds us therein." (PCUSA, 1989, 26)

Though new life in Christ occurs in and is shaped by accountability in a faith community, the Reformed tradition has emphasized the freedom and particularity of that life, meaning that it takes a specific form in the life of any individual. New life in Christ gets its "concrete shape" from the particular historical situation in which it is lived out.

The third qualification on organic or "natural" growth images for faithfulness from a Reformed perspective is the recognition of sin and mortality. The life of faith is not accurately described as slow but sure progress and development toward maturity, an innate quality that manifests over time. We often try to control or force our own growth in faith, or that of others, or someone imposes a specific definition of what new life in Christ is to be. Harmful and destructive forces within individuals, families, the church itself and other institutions, oppose and work against the creative and redemptive activity of God. Caregivers need to assess their own assumptions about how faith is fostered and to distinguish their own role and its limits, the role of the person to whom care is offered as response to God, and God's primary initiative in this process.

Fostering faithfulness is one way to think theologically about the purpose and meaning of pastoral visitation. Pastoral care is not only response to crises or identifiable needs, but also a means for affirming and nurturing response to grace in all circumstances. The integrity of caregivers may be demonstrated in their capacity to reflect biblical images of caregiving that broaden our understandings of God, clarify our sense of purpose in response to God, and discern the personal, social, and cultural factors that impede or oppose the work of God's grace. The following chapter builds on this exploration of a theology of visitation and suggests parables of the new creation and elements of pastoral conversation, which reflect this pastoral theological view.

Initial Steps in Pastoral Theological Reflection

Write down on your own, or discuss with a caregiver partner, your answers to the following questions:

1. Is your caregiving closer to shepherd, wounded healer, or wise fool? Are the strengths of this image similar to your own?

2. Is the understanding of God emphasized in this approach to giving care similar to your theological view of who God is? Experiment for at least one week with language that more broadly describes God.

3. Are the drawbacks or hazards in this approach to care demonstrated in your ministry of pastoral care? If so, what are two things you can do in your next visit to address these limits?

4. Which of the three images is underrepresented in your care? Identify and implement one small step you can take that moves toward fuller integration of a second biblical representation of care.

3

LEADING CONVERSATION—
A COLLABORATIVE APPROACH

The Sunday morning worship service included the sacrament of the Lord's Supper and, following worship, a lay leader and I took communion to older members who resided at a care center. Mrs. James had been a lifelong member of the church and seemed somewhat aware of us as we introduced ourselves and said why we were there. We talked a little about one of her great grandchildren who had been in church school class that morning. Then I took pieces of bread and three small cups from the communion kit, set them on her bedside table, and began to read the prayer of thanksgiving from the liturgy. Mrs. James interrupted twice with comments about the weather, apparently unable to comprehend that worship was in progress. But when I began the Lord's prayer, "Our Father, who art in heaven . . .," she began to say the prayer along with us, joining in word for word. We received the bread and the cup in memory of Christ's life, death, and resurrection, and in anticipation of all gathering at the table, from north and south and east and west, in the life to come.

In another congregation I served shortly after ordination, I went to visit Delmar in the hospital. He was a middle-aged man who suffered from a chronic, degenerative illness and was hospitalized from time to time for treatment of symptoms. He didn't attend worship and I hadn't met him before, but another member had warned me that he had some "sharp edges" and could be difficult. From the moment I walked in the hospital room I felt like I wanted to leave. He was angry with the nurses, the doctor, the hospital and, after I arrived, with God, the church and me. The pain medication was not working yet, and his doctor was in the process of changing it to find something that would work. But in the meantime, Delmar was expressing his distress to all within hearing distance. Though I tend toward tolerance of occasional swearing, I was taken aback by the sharpness of his curses at God, and really didn't know how to respond, except something like "I'm so sorry you're in such pain," several times. It was a short visit.

The next week, I got up my courage and visited Delmar at his mother's home where he lived. He was feeling better and glad to be out of the hospital. After I clarified for the second time that I was a pastor from his church, apparently a difficult concept, he began to talk about "this woman" who had visited him in the hospital but hadn't even offered to pray. When I realized who Delmar was talking about, I owned up and said, "That was me." I went on to explain that he had sounded so angry that it seemed like the last thing he would want, and so I'd decided not to ask if he wanted to pray. That was the last time I made that mistake as a pastor, and we ended that visit with a prayer.

Leading worship in the gathered community of faith is a definitive act of pastoral care, and not at odds with other one-to-one dimensions of care (Ramshaw, 1987, 13). The primary aim of worship is to glorify God. Ramshaw points out that the surest way to imbue one-on-one pastoral care with a sense of community and of the "transcendent" God is through conscious connection with the worship life of the community (1987, 14). The use of scripture and sacraments, and ritual worship in confession, declaration of pardon, thanksgiving and intercessory prayer, and blessing are among the vital forms of leadership in pastoral visitation.

A number of human needs are met through worship, including making sense of or "framing" experience, reaffirming meaning, bonding in community, handling mixed feelings, and encountering mystery (Ramshaw, 22–35). This is not to say that the primary purpose of worship is human comfort, but to acknowledge that needs are met in the process of liturgy and sacraments. Further, as Ramshaw points out, ritual worship can be "a force for justice," a power for order *and* for change, not of necessity removed from daily life, but helping people to imagine and to act in faithfulness to God's ongoing work. Worship can offer an alternative view of history and of the future, enacting a more just community of God's future in ritual form, and awakening desire for change in the present (Ramshaw, 88).

Use of ritual worship in visitation may seem beyond question, but some caution is warranted. Forms of worship should not be used as a substitute for a trusting relationship in pastoral care visitation, or because the caregiver is looking for an easy answer or a means of offering advice. Prayer is powerful when used appropriately, and it is best to ask rather than assume that it is welcome. Prayer during a visit can be most beneficial when generated in dialogue or shared with the other, and the caregiver may ask the person to suggest what they would like to have included in prayer. In this way, prayer is an act of community, generated in conversation and mutual relationship. Sometimes we help people to learn to pray again by praying with them during a visit. I do suggest that caregivers read prayers in the Book of Common Worship or similar resource books, reviewing what gifted writers have said in prayers for specific pastoral care situations (PCUSA, 1993). Advance preparation can be especially helpful for difficult or complicated circumstances, or when a caregiver's feelings are particularly strong because of the situation. But it is crucial to validate or reflect the person's perception of reality as understood from your conversation, *and* to affirm faith and realistic hope.

Use of scripture is appropriate in many types of pastoral visitation and, again, it is better to ask rather than to assume that the person would like to hear a passage. Biblical language and imagery may flow through dialogue within the circumstances of a particular pastoral care situation, and not just with the sick, dying, or bereaved (Gerkin, 1991, 114). Caregivers need to have in mind scripture readings that are familiar to many people (for example, Psalm 23, 27, 121, 139, John 14, Romans 8). For caregivers less familiar with scripture, appropriate passages for various types of visits can be identified in advance and noted on a card in the front cover of a Bible. Also, if a caregiver is not "well versed" in the Bible, don't ask if people have a favorite passage unless you're willing to struggle to find it in their presence, or ask for their help!

Exercising leadership as a good shepherd in pastoral visitation means providing opportunities for, but not coercing worship with those whom we visit. The form of worship may be brief and casual or much more structured and prolonged, but the purpose is to glorify God by claiming and giving thanks for our identity, in all circumstances, as the people of God, the body of Christ in the world, the community of the Spirit. When I failed to ask Delmar if we could pray when I visited him, I missed an opportunity to recall a different "order" or framework for his suffering, in the context of God's history and future. A simple prayer with him might have reaffirmed meaning and mystery in God's suffering love in the midst of understandably ambivalent or angry feelings. In Ramshaw's words, "This is neither cure nor answer (the resurrection does not erase the cross), it is at least a connection with the life of God hidden in our wounded lives" (1987, 65).

The moment of Mrs. James joining in the Lord's Prayer in the midst of the sacrament is an experience in visitation I hope all caregivers have, remembrance and foretaste of an alternative reality. The sacraments "make the promises of God palpable, give them form, flavor, wetness, and the warmth of human touch . . . [they] are the embodiment of the `already' element in the `already-not-yet' paradox of Christian eschatology" (Ramshaw, 1987, 95). I've known other such moments when a child adds to a prayer, or an elderly adult joins in singing a well-known hymn, just at the point I assumed they weren't listening or didn't understand, and God is glorified. The caregiver is both leader and participant.

RITUAL AUTHORITY AND POWER

"Woe to the shepherds who destroy and scatter the sheep of
my pasture!" says the Lord. Therefore thus says the Lord,
the God of Israel, concerning the shepherds who shepherd my people:
"It is you who have scattered my flock, and have
driven them away, and you have not attended to them. So I
will attend to you for your evil doings," says the Lord.
(Jer. 23:1-2)

Issues of power and authority, and the use of influence in pastoral conversation in visitation are central to a discussion of pastoral leadership.
Marie Fortune cited the preceding passage as she began addressing a
group of pastoral counselors on the issue of clergy misconduct (Fortune,
1989; Fortune and Poling, 1994). (Ethical conduct, tending boundaries in
relationship, and maintaining confidentiality will be addressed in chapter
5.) Commending leadership in the use of ritual forms of worship in visitation immediately involves the ambiguity of power and authority and
the potential for misuse.

One difficulty with the image of shepherd may be a presumption of
unequal power or influence between pastor and parishioner. While I do
not want to diminish the authority of the office of pastor, such inequity
in the dynamics of power can be hazardous and may contribute to mis-
judgments about how caregivers use power or influence with regard for
another's agency. As with most biblical images that inform pastoral care,
appropriate use of interpersonal influence and organizational power
becomes central in determining whether even well-intended care helps
or harms.

The appropriate use of interpersonal power and ecclesial authority
can be understood as a kind of "partnership" or authority "in community" (Russell, 1979, 1981, 1987). Partnership represents "a new focus of
relationship in which there is continuing commitment and common
struggle in interaction with a wider community context . . . a new focus
of relationship in a common history of Jesus Christ that sets persons
free for others" (Russell, 1979, 16). Russell defines power as the ability to
accomplish desired ends, and acknowledges that authority has often
been understood as power legitimated by the structures of society.

Using a sociohistorical perspective, Russell notes that authority in
Christian churches has usually been thought of as dominance, authority "over" community (1987, 87–99). The relational bond that usually
characterized authority in the Christian community was based on persons giving assent to another because they needed security in the
strength of others. The social relationships in this patriarchal under-

standing of authority take the shape of paternalism and autonomy, which "undercut more mature relationships of partnership" (1987, 89). Paternalism has been one form of domination, a relationship *without* a contract negotiated between equals, masked in the guise of love but leading to ongoing dependency. In autonomy, a second form of patriarchal authority, persons "exert power through projecting an appearance of superiority through the claim to complete self-sufficiency," a kind of authority without love (1987, 89). This type of authority projects an image of strength and invulnerability, authority needed by, but never needing others.

A different model of authority is found in Jesus' own ministry, in "koinonia" or partnership. Within this authority, bonds between people are those of assent, with people choosing to be in a two-way relationship of mutuality. Russell suggests that this form of authority is a gift of Christ's love, an interdependent relationship of trust and love, which remembers and anticipates the future new creation God brings. Such partnership does not imply complete equality, but "a pattern of equal regard and mutual acceptance of different gifts" (1987, 92).

The paternalistic, or to use a more gender-inclusive notion, a one-up, one-down approach, has been the most common form of authority for many caregivers. Trying to care for someone who does not attribute authority to the caregiver or who does not want the care offered, disregards the other's integrity. People are free to say "no" to care when it is offered. Some caregivers "teach" people to come to them so that their caring role is affirmed, when collaborating on behalf of people managing their own problem situations, or developing their unused resources and opportunities would be much more helpful (Egan, 1994, 160–70).

The "independent operators" who base authority on autonomy, deny the mutuality in caregiving and find it difficult to acknowledge what is received from those for whom they care. The "need to be needed" is a hazard for well-intended caregivers who enter a program of intentional visitation knowing that such ministry can be gratifying, but who lack the humility to receive, to be influenced by another's story or understanding of scripture, and who have difficulty welcoming interdependent relationship. Such helpers offer an inadvertent and theologically problematic dual message when they do not adequately perceive themselves as recipients of God's grace, and have difficulty appreciating the often startling generosity of people who "need" care.

Partnership is one way of understanding authority in pastoral visitation, which shifts the focus toward collaborative efforts. Unlike the mutuality or reciprocity of friendship, caregivers do not expect to receive what they are trying to give, but offer leadership, compassion, and perceptions in partnership as members of one body. In this way, caregivers take special responsibility but authority is attributed on the basis of a trustworthy pattern of behavior, sufficient self-awareness, and perception of God's redemptive presence. Such a caregiver does not overtake another's integrity or agency, does not function in isolation but as a member of a community of faith and accountability, providing the structure, space, and invitation for persons to address their needs. People are free to say "no" to this caregiver.

Earlier, I suggested that "pastoral" may be understood not as an ordained office or "the" leader of a church, but as a type of leadership, a use of power, a perspective based on wisdom. Ambiguity in the "official" status of caregivers in this book has been intentional in an effort to include ordained and lay caregivers, and to promote a broader understanding of pastoral care as an extension of the ministry of Jesus Christ, shared by all who claim to follow him. I am using the traditional biblical "pastoral," but reconsidering its meaning in the face of the ambiguity of power and the "qualified" authority that caregivers are sometimes granted.

A congregation that is less pastor-centered and more open to its immediate and wider, pluralistic context, needs concerned (and courageous) shepherds whose leadership and authority are based more on mutuality in relationships, regard for different views, and humility in following God into unknown territory. Pluralism has been defined as "diversity in culture, race, ethnicity, gender, and religion," a challenge and opportunity for renewal of the church, and an opportunity to rethink the gospel (Brueggemann and Stroup, 1998, 6). Theologian George Stroup suggests that one effect of pluralism is a shift in the church's understanding of its mission, from "taking God to a godless world" to "following God into a world in which God is already redemptively present" (1998, 8).

A congregation that is intentionally open and outward-focused in its pastoral visitation views pluralism as an opportunity, a means to the inner and interpersonal life of individuals, and interpret the influence of social and cultural factors at work. If the lay leader and I who visited Mrs. James had had concerns about the quality of her care, we would have spoken with her and her family about this concern (or directly to the care center staff if the need was urgent) We would have also addressed what, if any advocacy role they wanted us to play, and followed up to assure that the issue had been resolved. If I had heard Delmar express that one factor that exacerbated his suffering was a sense of failure because he had not married and raised a family or earned a living, roles his father had considered crucial for being a man, then we might have explored the detrimental influence of family and sociocultural expectations and perhaps opened a space for an alternative view.

Negotiating with persons for whom we care how they want caregivers to use authority or power is the collaborative approach of partnership. The courage to lead, a capacity for empathic understanding, and an alternative, wider perception of the person and sociocultural influences at work, strengthen not only the integrity of the caregiver, but the purpose of this relationship in the effective use of pastoral authority and power on behalf of another.

PARABLES FOR VISITATION

Going to see for the sake of relationships, inquiring about faith and fostering faith's practices, and encouraging and supporting others as they love and serve God in the interconnections of individual, congregation, and wider community—these essential purposes of visitation form the foundation in this book. Howard Stone has stated in his work on lay pastoral care that as its goal, pastoral conversation points the way toward a vision of the future shaped by the will of God and provides emotional support toward this different perspective (1991, 69–70).

Parables of the kingdom help us to recover biblical language and images, which shift the focus of pastoral visitation from an emphasis on the identity and integrity of the caregiver to include the collaboration or partnership of caregiver and careseeker. Parables of the "new creation," as I prefer to call them, help us to view pastoral visitation and the relationship of caregiver and careseeker in the ultimate context of what God is already doing. The metaphors of caregiving discussed in chapter 2 encourage integration of several strengths for caregivers, and help to identify potential hazards in various approaches to caring relationship.

In addition, I suggest that three biblical images of the new creation offer means for reconsidering the purpose of pastoral conversation and the type of relationship caregivers have with those we visit. Seed growing in the soil (Luke 8:4-8), yeast mixing in with flour (Luke 13:20), invitations to a great dinner already begun (Luke 14: 15-24)—these images help to recover and strengthen the purpose of visitation focused on nurturing relationship and fostering faithfulness. These kingdom parables may have originated in Jesus' response to his opponents who challenged his teaching that the kingdom was manifest at that time because they could not see it, and so didn't believe it.

> But the eyes and ears of faith saw and heard differently. As was the case with the story of the seeds sown, many of which did not produce, the final result will surprise. Or again, invited guests may have turned down the invitation, but the house will be full. The party will take place. . . . It is still

true that love and efforts for justice and peace seem paltry against the forces of human greed, fear and anger. . . . Yet the parable is heard to say that in the mystery of God's purpose and providence [the seeds] do yield. The little acts of caring that humans have to offer can bring surprising results. (Borsch, 1988, 122)

In the parable of the seeds, the growth that takes place is primarily the activity of God and we trust that what God has begun, God will inevitably complete. But this theme of the parable exists in tension with a call to active discipleship as we participate in the new creation begun in Jesus Christ. Christians live in the "in-between" time characterized by both waiting and action, given responsibility but not finally in charge, participating in "a mystery at work to which the secret of seeds alludes" (Borsch, 123–24).

Pastoral visits do not always reflect the new creation, and pastoral conversations do not of necessity include biblical language. Biblical metaphors for visitation offer a critical perspective of "otherness," suggesting alternate perceptions of reality, which the language of psychology or therapy does not provide (Gerkin, 1991, 114). Psychological theories provide categories for identifying intrapsychic and interpersonal dynamics, and psychotherapeutic theories and helping skills offer tools for addressing problems and implementing change—all marvelous contributions to the task of caregivers (see chapter 4). But such supporting disciplines do not displace the primary purpose of caregivers making pastoral visits and doing so on the basis of theological understandings and perceptions.

At the same time, "heavy-handed" use of biblical language or imagery may reduce the complexity of a care situation to a simplicity that falls short of metaphorical wisdom (Gerkin, 1991, 114). Parables of the new creation should not be used to reinforce a kind of Christian triumphalism.

> To be a believer is to follow the way of the parables . . . to live with the tension between the kingdom and the world, never identifying the one with the other while aware of the transformation of the world by the kingdom. . . . Religious people are less comfortable in the world, aware of the difference between things as they are and things as they ought to be; they are conscious of the metaphorical "is and is not." (McFague, 1982, 65)

Pastoral conversation holds in tension the "is and the is not" of our participation in the new creation, taking our place in the soil, in the mix of flour, and alongside other invited guests. The language of parables is indirect, it is a language of extravagance with elements of the extraordinary, of radicalism, of surprise and reversal; but the parables introduce this extravagance in mundane and ordinary stories about ordinary people making ordinary decisions (McFague, 1982, 44). The point of a parable is the play between "two descriptions of reality" which evoke "participatory thinking" (McFague, 1982, 46).

Three vignettes will illustrate pastoral conversations, which will then be explored on the basis of these parabolic images of what God has already begun and the kind of "participatory thinking" that results. The caregiver was visiting Sherry in her apartment, watching Sherry's eighteen-month-old son as he played on the floor. Sherry was a single parent who had attended worship twice in the past six months, and Linda was the Deacon who had been assigned by the pastor to visit. They had spoken after church on Sunday to arrange a time, and Linda knew from that conversation that Sherry was reluctant to commit herself to attending more often. Linda was also aware that Sherry had come to the church on weekdays several times to ask for assistance, and the pastor had given her food and a small amount of cash each time. Linda inquired about how long she had lived there (six months), whether she had friends or family in the area (a brother across the city), and asked whether she would consider joining one of the women's circles at the church.

SHERRY: I'm not really the joining kind, you know. I just wanted to see what it was like down there at the church, and I thought it would be good for Michael too.

LINDA: Well, we're glad you came to worship and want you to know you and Michael are welcome anytime. I know it's not easy to try to make friends in a new place.

SHERRY: That's the truth. I could use some friends, but I think I'm a little shy; mostly just keep to myself. I did see that sign about a school you have there at the church. I was thinking maybe Michael could get in there, be around some kids his own age. It would be good for him. But I don't have money for that, so I don't know.

LINDA: Yes, we do have a program three mornings a week for preschool age children. I'm not sure what the arrangements are for payment, but I could find out if they have openings and let you know.

SHERRY: Sounds good. I'd like Michael to be more outgoing than me. There is one thing, though, kind of embarrassing, but I've never been baptized. Is that a rule to have Michael there?

LINDA: Well, no, I'm sure it's not a rule for having a child there. I never thought about that before. It's an important step for you, though, I mean to be thinking about baptism. The only thing you have to do, as far as I know, is profess faith, not that that's a small thing. Is this what you've been thinking about?

SHERRY: Well, yeah. I've just been trying to get my life together, trying to do better by Michael, kind of make a fresh start here. I saw that sign for a school down at the church and thought that would be good for him. But, I don't know.

LINDA: You're not sure about . . .

SHERRY: I tried once before with a church and they didn't like it that I'd never married his father, you know. And I've just never felt like Michael was a big mistake or something. I just won't say that.

LINDA: That sounds awful . . . being asked to think that way about your son. I don't look at it that way. I mean you're here, and Michael's definitely here. Not that it's like anything goes, but it seems to me everyone's entitled to a fresh start.

SHERRY: Well, I'm trying.

LINDA: If I've understood you, getting Michael into a preschool group is important, and moving toward profession of faith and baptism is important, too, and you'll need some more information about that. Am I getting that right?

SHERRY: Yeah. Michael comes first, now.

This brief vignette invites many ways to think about it. One way of reflecting on this interaction, in the words of the parable, is that a seed had been planted long before Sherry came to worship at Linda's congregation, and somehow roots had taken hold. Sherry's effort to make a fresh start, her concern for her son, and her initiative in attending worship and seeking help from a church all signal growth despite conditions that could have overtaken that growth. Linda's role, in metaphorical terms of God's activity, was to affirm and nurture the growth that was already occurring, and perhaps to remain watchful and supportive with one whose agency in relation to rocks and weeds was gaining strength. Linda could have used some of the language of a parable or other scripture directly with Sherry, in simple terms of seed and soil, or the image of baptism, to evoke and add meaning to the story Sherry was telling. But doing so might have interrupted the dialogue rather than facilitating it. The following interaction includes more direct use of biblical language.

The pastor, Samuel, always enjoyed stopping to see Helen and found her to be one of the more "seasoned" members of the congregation, always in good humor. Helen was a retired high school teacher who volunteered at the women's center and shelter, and was currently serving on their board. As with many retirees, Samuel had to be sure to schedule a time to visit, or he wouldn't find her at home. Her husband had died ten years ago, and their daughter and her family lived in another state. They were seated in Helen's backyard, glasses of lemonade in hand.

HELEN: I'm not sure I can tolerate the new president of the board. All business, no heart. Maybe I'm too old and should just stay home!

SAMUEL: Not likely. [They laugh].

HELEN: Things have changed so much since I first started there. It was quite a ride getting that shelter started twenty years ago. This year there's a black tie fundraiser at the country club. I wouldn't be caught dead at it. It's a good cause that's been compromised in order to survive.

SAMUEL: I haven't heard you sound this discouraged before.

HELEN: I do feel discouraged, at least today. But then I hear one more story or meet one more family who needs a safe place to stay and I stick with it. Oh, enough about me, what's going on with you?

Samuel: I'm doing fine. You know, you are effective on that board, though. Reminds me of the leaven in the loaf . . . it gets mixed in and mixed in and, . . .

HELEN: Oh no, it's flat bread!

SAMUEL: Very funny.

HELEN: Thanks.

SAMUEL: But you're in the mix on that board, and I think you liked it better when there was a more casual approach. Most everyone saw things your way, so it didn't feel like hard work, so discouraging.

HELEN: That's true. It was more fun. We liked each other. We felt a camaraderie in that hand-to-mouth time that isn't there anymore. Sounds a little self-righteous, doesn't it?

SAMUEL: Nostalgic, maybe.

HELEN: No, self-righteous. I forget who's in charge here, or it feels like nobody's in charge here, just operating a business. That's when I get discouraged. Just need to find my place again and not worry that it's all mine to do, my way.

The biblical language is used in this illustration in a light-hearted, rather than a heavy-handed manner. Apart from Samuel's "official" status in the church, consider what was "pastoral" in this conversation. First, trust and mutual respect abound in this relationship, built over a period of time and many interactions. Mention of the parable about God's dominion brings a different perspective on Helen's discouragement as a board member and calls into question whether she is taking too much responsibility for the "leaven" in a just cause. Through this interaction

Helen comes to her own conclusion about what she needs in the face of discouragement, a reminder of God's ongoing "leavening" activity in the world, and our relative influence in the mix.

COLLABORATIVE CONVERSATION

Pastoral conversation has been understood as an art often associated with attention to the "inner" spiritual growth of individuals (Faber and van der Schoot, 1965; Noyce, 1981).

Research on helping skills indicates that the best predictor of "success" in a helping process is the quality of the relationship, more than any theory employed (Egan, 1994). Going to see someone as a caregiver involves taking the initiative, clarifying the purpose, taking into consideration the circumstances of the person. Leading a pastoral conversation during a visit requires skills in building a relationship and providing a safe interpersonal space, using active listening skills and empathic responses that offer an emotional resonance for conversation, and structuring the interaction toward "collaborative conversation." A key element in this structure is the ability to take an opportunity or to open a space for fostering faith in the process of this interaction. Other skills for visitation will be discussed in chapter 4, but the focus in what follows is appropriate use of ritual authority and opening space for collaborative conversation.

I have set aside discussion of particular therapeutic theory in this project in order to gain a fuller view not only of the integrity of the caregiver, but of caregiving as a situation in which God is already redemptively at work. The insights and skills offered in psychological and therapeutic theories must be shaped through collaborative conversation for the purpose of anticipating and participating in the work of the coming kingdom, the new creation. Such participation is not only a question of the caregiver's identity and integrity, but also a more thorough understanding of the parabolic setting of care as rocky soil for a seed, as mixture of leaven and flour, and as guests ambivalent about their invitations to a dinner.

I admit to quite a difference between the conversations I had as a pastor with parishioners and those I have as pastoral counselor with clients, and to some extent that is as it should be. One difference is my hesitance in claiming and using ritual authority in a more specialized, clinical setting. Sometimes I wonder if I have not lost my pastoral identity, so much as the broader pastoral purpose of offering care and counseling in aligning with what God is calling forth in some alternative perception of reality as God's love and justice.

On the other hand, some very good reasons explain why I do not pray with some clients. They do not necessarily acknowledge my pastoral authority, and we do not often share a language of faith so fully as when I functioned as a pastor. We do not share experiences of corporate worship or fellowship and mission in the life of a community of faith, and so the language of faith seems almost intrusive, interrupting the conversation rather than facilitating it. But if "pastoral" has more to do with the purpose of this interaction than with the identity of the caregiver, a way may be found to foster faithfulness to God who is, even now, bringing creation to fullness and completion. Pastoral conversation as it was understood in the work of Faber and van der Schoot drew from the work of Carl Rogers's client-centered approach in psychotherapy (Faber and van der Schoot, 1965; Rogers, 1951). Empathy was a basic element of this conversation, as was unconditional positive regard for and acceptance of the person seeking care. In addition, the genuineness and authenticity of the caregiver was paramount, communicating openness and warmth that invited trust and disclosure in the conversation. I have heard it said many times that it is hard to go wrong using such an approach in pastoral care, and I still agree. This description of pastoral conversation parallels the most basic helping skills based on attending and listening, communicating empathy, helping the person identify and clarify problem situations, create a better future, and implement their goals (Egan, 1994). And yet, does pastoral caring involve more than these elements of conversation?

> We sense that the work of preaching, teaching, pastoral care, and pastoral counseling has responsibilities for proclamation and interpretation of the faith unfulfilled by Rogerian habits of empathic listening alone.... While liberation may not be adequate as a summary motif of the church's mission and derivative leadership roles, it does hold out for us a more active overarching image than shepherding and counseling. We are also preachers, liturgists, teachers, and community organizers; and we hope conceptually to keep all these together in a viable discipleship. (Noyce, 1981, 45ff)

Pastoral theologian Gaylord Noyce discusses pastoral conversation in terms of the "nondirective handicap" (Noyce, 1981). Cultural elements hinder more active proclamation and interpretation of faith in pastoral conversation. Noyce states that the element of privatism, if exaggerated, would mean that values, commitments, and beliefs should not be urged on anyone by anyone else (1981, 37). Noyce views "cheap religious talk" as an additional difficulty, when God is named so often that all sense of God's "holiness" is lost. In such instances, a simple word of compassion would have been a better vehicle of proclamation than "God-talk" because it could have been heard.

However, avoidance of "God-talk" may become such a habit that we do not speak of our faith convictions at all. "Fear of controversy" may also hinder giving voice to faith, as when a person has not yet learned to say "I think we disagree on that," or "It sounds like we see that differently." Noyce went on to suggest, nearly twenty years ago, that an emerging language of spirituality held promise for practicing "articulate exchange" in matters of faith (1981, 136). A focus on spirituality is certainly one direction that some pastoral conversation has taken in an effort to talk about faith in terms of service and practice of spirituality, without engaging in "cheap talk" about God.

But another way of looking at pastoral visitation in a pluralistic culture is that elements of the culture—historicism, materialism, privatism—call for "testimony" to a different way of seeing, an alternative interpretation, opening a new possibility (Hoyt, 1997). In the parable of the great dinner the possibility of accompanying other guests to the banquet involves engaging those who are too busy to accept that invitation. One way of inviting conversation about faith, calibrating one's approach between too aggressive and too passive, is *to focus on practices of faith* to which we are all called. Pastoral visitation shaped around this focus, provides caregivers a means for "opening" talk about faith in a way that is not intrusive, and offers a different view of the "dailiness" of faith.

Specific practices of faith are discussed by a number of authors in a work edited by Dorothy Bass: honoring the body, hospitality, household economics, saying yes and saying no, keeping sabbath, testimony, discernment, shaping communities, forgiveness, healing, dying well, and singing our lives (Bass, 1997). A description of such practices, particularly if mailed in advance of a visit, could provide ample points at which to open conversation.

> Ask people to discuss a practice in the concreteness of their own lives, and you will find it hard to stop the conversation. What would it really mean to practice forgiveness in this situation? What is your favorite hymn? What "no" does our family have to say in order to say an important "yes"? Do we live in a society that honors the human body? How should I discern the right thing to do? Have you known anyone who died well? . . . Ask about practices, and stories tumble out. Tears and laughter erupt. Connections get made. People talk, and people listen. (Bass, 1997, 195)

Another resource for opening mutual, collaborative conversation about practices of faith identifies practices and disciplines from my own tradition:

1. worshiping God together;
2. telling the Christian story to one another;
3. interpreting together the scriptures and the history of the church's experience in relation to their meaning for our own lives;

4. praying together and by ourselves;

5. confessing sin to one another, forgiving, and becoming reconciled;

6. tolerating one another's failures and encouraging one another in the work each must do and the vocation each must live;

7. carrying out specific faithful acts of service together;

8. suffering with and for each other and all whom Jesus showed us to be our neighbors;

9. providing hospitality and care to one another and to strangers;

10. listening and talking attentively to one another about our particular experiences in life;

11. struggling together to become conscious of and understand the nature of the context in which we live;

12. criticizing and resisting all those powers and patterns (both within the church and in the world as a whole) that destroy human beings, corrode human community, and injure God's creation;

13. working together to maintain and create social structures and institutions that will sustain life in the world in ways that accord with God's will (PCUSA, 1989).

Such a list of faith practices for reflection, sent in advance of a visit, can become a focus in a noncrisis type of pastoral conversation when fostering faith is a primary purpose. Collaborative conversation on such a topic involves building a relationship of trust, communicating understanding through active, empathic listening, and using the person's own words, images, or strong feelings to explore what, if anything, they would like to change. But the crucial feature is to take an opportunity when it appears for speaking of faithfulness, or to open an opportunity for exploration of faith practices, and in this way to lead the conversation. Examples of such openings would include: I'm wondering what, if anything, surprised you as you looked through this list? Which of these practices comes most easily for you? Which would be most challenging? What factors in your life support your practices of faith? What makes them difficult? In collaborative relationship, such starting points lead to talk about faith and open the possibility for constructive change and fuller practice of faith.

Stories of daily, even "ordinary" faithfulness are the focus of collaborative pastoral conversation, just as biblical parables and stories were found to be the best way to understand the mystery of God's presence and absence in daily life. Understanding this mystery was often done by telling a story in two different ways—

> by presenting two versions of a story—one in which we hear of human adventures and foibles without any mention of God, another in which God is at least just offstage if not directly involved in the action. . . .

Through human character and dialogue, through those seeking God's will and failing to find it, and others denying it yet being led by it, through repeated basic plot themes and the counterpoint of plots, the audience is induced by means of narrative to explore the significance of life lived before God. (Borsch, 1988, 4)

Pastoral conversation may indeed mean commenting on another version of the story that's been heard during a visit, proclaiming and interpreting in a nonauthoritarian, collaborative manner, the version with God just offstage or even front and center. Such conversation also occurs when the caregiver hears awareness of God's presence or absence in another's story, and helps to identify what small step of faith will be taken in the face of this mystery.

Collaborative pastoral conversation is one-to-one but also "wider" conversation that lifts up interconnections among individuals, congregations, and their community. In his work on improving quality of life and health in local communities, Gary Gunderson views a congregation as a vital link between personal, private spirituality and social factors that affect wider community life (1997, 19). He discusses eight strengths of congregations for this task: to accompany, convene, connect, give sanctuary and context, to bless, pray, and persist. Although all these strengths have implications for visitation, one in particular serves to highlight the strong "position" of a congregation in its community, a position that can be strengthened through pastoral conversation in visitation. Gunderson describes a congregation as "building patterns of accompaniment," viewing the congregation as the link between personal spirituality and the social factors that affect the life of a congregation.

For instance, creating helping roles that make it easier for people to voluntarily engage those who may be outside of their normal range of vision, or infusing other community structures with healthy social expectations—these are among the patterns of accompaniment Gunderson suggests. In this way, a congregation is a kind of "force field" in which its strengths become channels "along which we can expect to find God breaking into our midst and nurturing our communities toward life" (Gunderson, 1997, 22).

Most programs of visitation are designed to serve the members and friends of the local church with some purpose of organizational maintenance and development in mind. For some churches, any program is concerned with the survival of the institution, and so contacting members and prospective members, and nurturing these relationships, is a crucial component of ensuring the survival of that particular community of faith. The congregational strength of accompaniment can be congruent with survival and maintenance needs when it is identified and encouraged in pastoral conversation as practice of faith. Accompaniment affirms the unique opportunity for congregations to engage in "wider" collaborative conversations and actions in their communities. This larger understanding of pastoral conversation leads to a more accurate rendering of the biblical term *pastoral* as a perspective in congregations that seek and celebrate collaborative interconnections. Leading conversation during a pastoral visit means effective use of helping skills, which builds a relationship of trust by communicating understanding through active listening and structuring the dialogue in a collaborative manner.

Faith "talk" is not a requirement for all pastoral visitation and can be presumptive or intrusive in a situation where another urgent agenda requires attention, or when a safe interpersonal space and mutual trust have not been sufficiently established. Scripture and ritual forms of worship are also not automatically included in the course of a pastoral visit if doing so would trivialize their power or violate the purpose of these elements of pastoral care. But worship, scripture, and opening space for conversation about faith are powerful, paradigmatic acts of care that can frame experience in God's history, present activity, and future. Leading conversation connects and reconnects people with their faith community and the larger life of God.

Steps to Action

1. List the practices of faith in which you currently engage, noting the two that are most important to you.

2. Find a partner or a group of caregivers with whom you can practice pastoral conversation in roleplays. Secure a video camera, VCR, and monitor, and tape the roleplays if at all possible.

3. Roleplay a brief (five minute) portion of pastoral conversation with a partner in which the caregiver inquires, directly, about one current practice of faith. Listen for the person's words, images, strong feelings, or key experiences and explore them further.

4. Experiment in the roleplay with both heavy-handed and light-hearted references to scripture and identify how it feels to you, as a caregiver, to include explicit references in conversation. Receive feedback from the partner about how the scripture reference fit or didn't fit.

5. In the roleplay, lift up any interconnections you hear, which link a practice of faith with a person's family or network of friends, the life of the congregation, actions in the local community, or expression of faith in wider social and political concerns.

6. View the roleplays (if videotaped) with your partner or as a group

and hear from both caregiver and careseeker how it felt to participate in this brief interaction. Identify the strengths of the caregiver and discuss the leadership that was offered and any elements of collaboration or partnership evident in the interchange. Share constructive critical comments on what might have happened differently to strengthen the interchange as pastoral conversation.

4

EQUIPPING CAREGIVERS— HELPING SKILLS

Returning to one of the vignettes from chapter 1, we recall the caregiver who visited Al at the nursing home and listened as Al remembered his wife Betsy and talked about favorite baseball teams. The conversation continued.

HENRY: You know, I can't help admiring how you've gone on with your life after your wife died. It's hard for me to imagine what that would be like, losing someone so close.

AL: It wasn't easy, I'll tell you. It wasn't easy. And then moving here. But you know we had a good life. And our son has done real well. That makes it a little easier.

HENRY: You've been able to get through some rough places along the way, and still keep going.

AL: I've managed all right. God has been real good to me, if I do say so.

HENRY: If I remember, this is the third time I've come to see you, and every time you talk about what you're thankful for, the good things in your life. When I leave, I think, what have I got to complain about? I think you're good for me, Al, a good influence.

AL: Well, maybe the guy up there has something to do with it. He's always come through for me, just like the Bible says, so I can't complain. Besides I'm headed for home plate, as far as I know.

HENRY: If you don't mind my asking, what helped the most when you lost Betsy? I mean, I visit other folks who just never get through it, and I'd like to know what helped you keep going on.

AL: Well, I wasn't alone. Other people were hurting too when Betsy passed. You can't go through it alone. But if I start to feel bad, I see who's around, or better yet, get someone to watch a game with me. You've got to try. I mean God can only do so much, and then it's up to you.

HENRY: So God is with you, but you help yourself too, so you don't sink too low. Well, I wish everybody had that attitude. To tell the truth, I could probably use some attitude adjustment myself along those lines.

AL: You mean you get too lonesome?

HENRY: Well not lonesome so much as just worn out with work and the kids and all. But coming to visit you makes me think more about where

I'm headed, somewhere between first and second base, I think! I've got a lot to be thankful for. You know what I mean?

AL: Yeah, you've got to try and keep that straight, get things in the right order, that's for sure. Life is short.

When Henry was concluding the visit, he asked Al if he'd like prayer together. They both took part.

This brief, rather straightforward visit illustrates several things about the skills needed for pastoral visitation. First, a level of trust in the relationship has been built through several interactions in which the caregiver's behavior has been attentive and empathic. Henry listened carefully to what Al was saying, and stayed with Al's descriptions of his experience, reflecting accurately what had been said. Even when Henry inquired about what had helped Al the most, a question in which he had personal interest, it was not an agenda that displaced the flow of conversation, but fostered Al's further reflection.

One of the gifts this caregiver offered was direct, affirming feedback about the influence Al was having on him. Affirmation of this sort can feel especially helpful for someone whose interactions may be limited in number and intimacy. Henry made it clear that he was learning something important with Al. Reflecting on the situation as a pastoral caregiver, one might suggest that the Spirit had brought about something new, an affirmation that supports and encourages Al's continued faithfulness. Further, such a visit does not focus on a problem to be resolved so much as it enhances health and strength that already exist, which takes the form of care and prevents suffering. The element of collaborative, mutual influence is clear in the interchange, both giving, both receiving, which is the "leavening" at its best.

If some difference between these two men had been sharper, a more dramatic difference in capacities to trust, in age, race or ethnicity, sex, economic class, employment or educational background, sexual orientation, or if their religious views and theological assumptions had clashed, the dynamics in this interchange would have been more complex, but *not necessarily more difficult.* Differences become distorted through biased and prejudiced views that attribute power, or even opposition on the basis of being unlike another person in age, race, sex, or economic class, and the like. Good listening becomes much more difficult if caregivers assume they hear someone well because they are "like" the person in many ways, or if they assume they can't understand or be helpful to someone who is "unlike" them. Caregivers must be diligent to work through bias and prejudice within themselves so that differences are encountered with regard and respect rather than assumptions of superiority or inferiority (Augsburger, 1986; Graham, 1992; Hollies, 1991;

Marshall, 1997; Moessner, 1996; Neuger, 1996; Poling and Neuger, 1996; van Beek, 1998; Wimberly, 1991).

Some visits will require skill in managing conflict among family members or between the caregiver and careseeker. Experience in hearing complaints in a nondefensive manner will increase a caregiver's ability to respond effectively by finding some point of agreement with the careseeker, offering empathic responses, and asking for more information on their experience (Miller and Jackson, 1995). Development of basic listening skills will enable the caregiver to formulate the problem in terms that identify goals for change and at least tentative, partial resolution.

In addition to a habit of theological reflection and leading conversation in a collaborative manner, caregivers need to be skilled at listening and capable of observing and assessing accurately enough to respond effectively in a particular situation of care. Helping skills for pastoral visitation include attending behaviors that build trust, active listening, empathic responses and judicious use of questions, and assessment of what is going on, what problems need to be addressed, or growth encouraged. Caregivers are responsible for structuring the interaction to include an introduction, a purposeful dialogue, and a predicted conclusion. Certain skills are required to decide whether consultation is needed, and in knowing when and how to refer for additional help.

Listening skills can be taught and learned among caregivers open to increasing self-awareness, altering their own problematic patterns of interaction, and continuing to enhance skills. Many caregivers claim a kind of "intuitive" sense for pastoral caring, which is wonderful as long as it isn't considered superior to or doesn't take the place of skilled and "informed" care. The variety of gifts among members of the body of Christ is one good reason to encourage lay caregiving. Numerous resources offer discussions on basic helping skills (Brammer, 1988; Clinebell, 1984; Egan, 1994; Miller and Jackson, 1995; Ivey et al., 1997). Some congregations choose to use structured training opportunities such as Stephen Ministries in order to equip caregivers and to meet needs for visitation. Howard Stone's work using a brief therapy approach in pastoral care and counseling is particularly effective in addressing particular needs in a short period of time (1994). In addition, numerous works in solution-focused therapy and brief therapy offer theory and illustrations of practice that can greatly enhance the ministry of caregiving (O'Hanlon and Weiner-Davis, 1989; Walter and Peller, 1992).

Obviously the skills and theory base for pastoral visitation will vary widely depending on the congregation and its needs. But the relation of theory and practice in caregiving is an ongoing process of integrating skills and information into one's primary identity as a theologian.

Reflecting on experience in caregiving ministry, discerning what additional skills and information are needed, and deciding what theological assumptions or commitments fit or don't fit any longer, is a process driven not by therapeutic theory but by theological purpose, reflecting and anticipating the love and justice of God.

ACTIVE LISTENING

Skilled listening takes practice. Perhaps the most important element, skill in reflective listening, serves to clarify understanding. Reflective listening means actively and accurately mirroring the person's thoughts and feelings, insights and conflicts, giving back an undistorted image of the speaker's meaning (Miller and Jackson, 1995, 54). Because the listener reflects meaning, not just statements made, the annoying mistake of "parroting" back exactly what was said is avoided. Instead, the listener reflects, as much as possible, an *understanding* of what was heard, knowing that the speaker's intended meaning and what was stated in words (meaning "encoded") are often different. Further, as Miller and Jackson point out, what the listener heard and "decoded"—the listener's interpretation of the speaker's intended meaning— is an added difference.

Most people assume that they know what the speaker meant and respond on that basis. "Reflective thinking makes this process conscious, reminding you that your interpretation is only a guess and may not match what was actually meant" (Miller and Jackson, 1995, 57). In other words, the listening skill needed in caregiving involves some guessing, considering different possible meanings, as well as a variety of intentions, thoughts, and feelings in what a person says.

Levels of Reflection

Three levels of reflection can be identified and used in combination by skillful listeners: simple repetition, partial rephrasing, and whole paraphrase, adding meaning (Miller and Jackson, 1995, 61). The purpose of reflecting is not only an accurate guess, although it is the place we start, but the use of some partial rephrasing and occasional paraphrasing adds meaning to what was heard. For instance, when Henry was visiting Al, he responded, "You've been able to get through some rough places along the way and still keep going." This response demonstrates partial rephrasing based on Henry's perception and admiration of Al's ability to "keep going" in the face of loss and change. Henry could have made a response using simple repetition, such as "It hasn't been easy losing Betsy and moving here, but life has been good, and that helps." A response using whole paraphrasing, adding meaning might be, "So even though it's been very difficult, you're thankful for your life with Betsy and for your son, and this attitude helps you to make the most of life now." Suggesting that Al is "thankful" adds a meaningful interpretation of his experience, framing it in terms of relationship with God. The reflective response—"making the most of life now"—implies that Henry's thankfulness brings a measure of fullness to his life now. When Henry responded, "So God is with you, but you help yourself too, so you don't sink too low," he used simple repetition, affirming Al's sense of God's active presence and Al's agency on his own behalf, a kind of preventive self-care because "sinking too low" remains a possibility. A response using partial rephrasing might have followed, emphasizing God's action in Al's life and exploring how this happens for him: "From what I can see, you try and it works. God's given a lot to you, but then it's your responsibility." A whole paraphrase response adding more meaning could have been: "Your faith sounds so strong. I can't help wondering if that's what makes the difference for you, Al. You seem to feel that God cares about you, like most of us do, but for you it seems to make more of a difference."

As a caregiver, Henry opened an opportunity when he posed the question: "If you don't mind my asking, what helped the most when you lost Betsy?" The question could have been out of personal curiosity, but it served to invite Al to identify what has been at work that helped (and continues to help) him endure in the face of loss. Al's notion of community confirms the idea that people who grieve are most likely to believe God knows their pain if they experience others who are willing to suffer with them (Mitchell and Anderson, 1983, 169).

Henry recalled Al's baseball analogy, and reintroduced this image in his response, "Coming to visit you makes me think more about where I'm headed, somewhere between first and second base, I think. I've got a lot to be thankful for." The conversation between Al and Henry is flowing well, and Henry demonstrates good listening skills in returning to this analogy for life itself. Listening for images or analogies offered by the person, and inquiring about them in an open-ended, "tell me more about . . ." approach is part of the "art of understanding" in pastoral care.

Phases of a Care Process

The structure of a pastoral care process can be understood from a psychological view as occurring in four phases: (1) clarification as the art of understanding, (2) formulation as the art of thinking clearly, (3) intervention as making a difference, drawing from information on specific problem areas, and (4) termination with continued pastoring and support (Miller and Jackson, 1995). As with most work in pastoral care and counseling, Miller and Jackson's approach focuses on helping persons to identify problems and formulate plans for addressing them: mood, grief, depression, suicide, stress and anxiety, anger and aggression, misuse of alcohol and drugs, addiction, major mental disorders, and relationship counseling.

In this discussion of pastoral visitation, I concentrate on visitation and conversation with persons who do not necessarily have identifiable "problems," per se, although these issues may certainly emerge in the process. Some excellent material addresses specific problems, which I will not attempt to duplicate here (Capps, 1993; Clinebell, 1984, 1998; Graham, 1992; Lester and Lester, 1998; Marshall, 1997; Miller-McLemore, 1994; Mitchell and Anderson, 1983; Moessner, 1996; Penner and Penner, 1981; Poling and Neuger, 1996; Rando, 1984; Stone, 1998; Stone and Clements, 1991; Wicks et al., 1993). Here, we will use the structure of Miller and Jackson's framework in practical psychology to identify listening skills for visitation so that caregivers use "systematic yet flexible thinking" to address problems or encourage growth in a process of care. In collaborative pastoral conversation, dialogue may range widely but often focuses on the immediacy of life in stories of family, home, health, school, or work. Asking what is going well for people or what they are enjoying in any of these dimensions can be beneficial.

Defining a Problem or Area for Growth

One way for caregivers to help others define problems or areas for growth is to keep in mind four questions that may structure a process of care: What is troubling the person? What is causing the problem? What is missing? and What is needed? (Miller and Jackson, 1995). Though not intended to be asked directly of the careseeker, these four questions help caregivers to organize their thoughts while listening during a visit or reflecting on one later. The first question considers three domains of experience—affect, behavior, and cognition—and identifying how the domains interact and conflict in the person's problem situation or desired growth. The second question includes "types" of causes for a problem or impediment to growth: primary, predisposing, precipitating, and perpetuating causes, looking not only at where the problem or hindrance began, but what keeps it going now.

The third question for caregivers to keep in mind looks at the problem or potential growth area from a broader view of the person's life, and asks what the person seems to be lacking or avoiding. The question of what is missing, or what one has "too little of" in life, is examined in terms of experiencing fulfillment in three areas—work, relationships, and aloneness. These areas can be framed as theological issues: (1) "doing," or adequate sense of vocation, (2) "moving" toward or away from others in a network of relationships that sustain and endure, and (3) the existential notion of "being" and identity, with attention to, but not preoccupation with "internal" reality. Caregivers listen for the *balance* among these three areas of life—doing, moving in relation to others, and being—and adequate sense of *fulfillment* in each.

Identifying a Goal

The final question caregivers consider in this psychological framework is what is needed, and moves toward the last phase of the process, which is intervention. The answer to what is needed may become obvious through consideration of the first three questions, but can be identified in three different possible goals for the caregiving process: change, choice, or confusion reduction. The first possible goal may involve any of the three domains of experience (affect, behavior, cognition) or any or all of the areas of fulfillment (work, relationships, aloneness). The second possible goal, making a choice, often involves the issue of readiness for change in a conflicted situation. The goal of caregiving then becomes making a decision. The third possible goal focuses on confusion reduction, particularly if a person's "cognitive structure," the perspective and unspoken rules by which they have lived, have been shattered or called into question. A person experiencing such confusion is not prepared for change or choice, and so the goal becomes restructuring, integration, and regaining a perspective.

Caregivers must decide whether to proceed in addressing a need, or to shift toward referral and even persuasion in guiding someone to the help they need. Identifying the limits of one's competency becomes an ethical issue for caregivers, and using consultation is one way to help make decisions about how to proceed in a specific situation of care (Miller and Jackson, 1995, 31–32). I strongly encourage pastors to identify and contract with a consultant in their vicinity, though not in their congregation. This consultant may be a pastoral counselor, psychologist, therapist, or social worker licensed by the state. Sometimes a local church will consider budgeting for this contract in order to provide the support and resources for the pastor and lay caregivers. It may be a contract on an "as needed" basis, or it may be a once-a-month review of care and counseling situations to evaluate and improve effectiveness in ministry.

Considering Referral

Psychiatrist Dana Charry has identified five groups of persons who should be referred for additional help by clergy and other caregivers: (1) persons who are psychotic, out of touch with reality; (2) people who are overtly suicidal or who have a history of attempts; (3) people with significant addiction and substance abuse problems; (4) those who show signs of severe depression, which interferes with their physical functioning and daily activities; and (5) people who show signs of brain disease such as confusion or disorientation (Charry, 1981, 18).

I encourage caregivers to prepare a referral resources list in their context of ministry in advance of need, and then continue developing these resources. Locating persons, agencies, and services to whom you can refer with confidence is crucial. Sometimes information can be gained over the phone, but particularly with potential referral resource persons such as a pastoral counselor, psychiatrist, psychologist, social worker, marriage and family therapist, or drug and alcohol counselor, it is better to meet the person, even briefly, to discuss their particular areas of interest or expertise.

An important goal of a referral centers on a smooth transition to include this additional help (Miller and Jackson, 1995, 425–34). Preparation and "maintenance" of this kind of network in advance of an urgent need helps with the transition and strengthens one's own sense of interconnection in the community. Care must be taken in explaining the reason for a referral, and clarifying what the role of the caregiver will be after the referral occurs. If at all possible, the referral should be specific, and knowledge of the person or agency helps in addressing concerns about the nature, cost, and duration of the service that is recommended.

PASTORAL ASSESSMENT

Recalling the vignette from chapter 1, Pastor Sally visited Melissa a second time while she was at the drug rehabilitation facility for two weeks. Sally had spoken with Melissa's parents by phone since she last visited Melissa, and they said they felt hopeful about her treatment and progress, but were concerned that not enough had changed. When Sally talked directly with Melissa on the phone, Melissa said she could meet with Sally after school at home. Melissa's parents would not be home yet from work, but Sally decided to go ahead, assuming that Melissa wanted to talk without her parents present. When Sally visited, they talked about what the past two weeks had been like for Melissa, some difficulties she had with her roommate, and the conversation continued.

SALLY: So other than problems in sharing a room, it sounds like the treatment worked, that you've gotten some of what you needed.

MELISSA: Some of it helped. The group was really boring sometimes, but, you know, it was different to hear other kids talk about messing up too. I wasn't the only one who made bad choices.

SALLY: You mean that you heard other kids talk more openly about their problems there, in the group?

MELISSA: Yeah, a lot more open. I mean it was weird in a way, but cool, too, hearing them talk about everything, I mean everything.

SALLY: And you were able to open up, too, in the group?

MELISSA: Kind of. I did say a lot more about what made me do it, you know, smoking some pot and then trying "coke."

SALLY: I'm glad you were able to talk about it there. So you figured out some ways to make different choices, to get on a different track?

MELISSA: Right. Nick, the therapist, worked on that a lot. He kept asking about the people and the places that were bad influences, and what other options we had. We had to write them down and read them to the group, like a self-defense plan, we called it.

SALLY: It sounds like you worked on a plan, setting yourself up to succeed. I'd be interested in what you came up with, if it's something you want to say more about.

MELISSA: Sure. . . . [she describes a thought-stopping process.]

SALLY: I'm glad you wanted to talk with me again, and we can continue to do this. I'd like to be supportive, not that I'd take the place of any of the after-care plan you've worked out. But I'm wondering what you would like from me in this process?

Most caregivers need a structured approach to an assessment process in order to listen well and to gain a full and accurate picture of the situation. It does not necessarily mean one needs to sit with pencil and paper in hand, but on some occasions it may. The purpose of pastoral assessment is to enhance ministry by accurately identifying problems and needs in the spiritual lives of people with whom we work (Fitchett, 1993). Assessment helps caregivers set goals for ministry rather than responding merely in a spontaneous or impulsive manner.

Assessment in pastoral visitation includes psychologically informed definition of problem situations and areas for growth, but some caregivers need a broader type of inventory for more systematic assessment. Moving beyond a psychological framework, caregivers can also listen *"into" the conversation for echoes of a wide range of biblical and theological themes:* confession and repentance, grace and reconciliation, doxology and thanksgiving, blessing and joy, presence in lament and suffering, comfort in loss and grief, healing and wholeness, injustice and oppressive circumstances, freedom and liberation, community and companionship, alienation or isolation, generativity and caring for others, covenants, commitments and sexuality, vocation and work (Clinebell, 1984, 74–78; Oates, 1982, 167–89; Miller and Jackson, 1995, 44–74). Such "thematic" listening moves toward fuller pastoral assessment of theological issues in a person's story, as an opportunity for further exploration (Lester, 1995; Capps, 1990, 1998).

Pastoral assessment occurs during a visit through active listening, and in reflection following a visit using a more systematic list or inventory, such as the list of theological themes stated in the preceding paragraph. Reflection may also be guided by the enduring efforts of Draper (1965) and Pruyser (1976), and more recently, Fitchett (1993) and Ramsey (1998). Pruyser, a clinical psychologist, identified seven variables for pastoral diagnosis and strongly encouraged pastors to recover their religious language. Wayne Oates drew from Draper and Pruyser's "patterns of spiritual inquiry" in his discussion of pastoral assessment (1982, 180–87), as did George Fitchett in developing a holistic assessment model.[11]

A summary of Pruyser's religious themes and Oates's addition of the "dark side" of these themes may be paraphrased as follows:

1. Explore the person's awareness of the holy—and its darker counterpart in the sense of the "devil, the uncanny, the eerie, and the weird" (Oates, 1982, 187).

2. Explore the person's awareness of providence—and how it may be beleaguered by feelings of fate, bad luck, or being cursed.

3. Search with the person for the subjective experience of faith—and the ways in which it is stalemated by discouragement, fear, and anxiety.

4. Probe the person's sense of grace or gratefulness—as over against legalism, perfectionism, and compulsive guilt.

5. Meditate with the person about times of repenting that the person may have been through—and when this repentance has been frustrated by a spirit of "unforgiveness" and hardness of heart.

6. Get in touch with the person's sense of communion—and the loneliness that may work against it.

7. Explore the person's sense of vocation—and the ways in which "fine resolve and fantasy of total success" prevent a person from responding to God's purposes.

This type of list may be used to reflect more thoroughly on one pastoral care situation each week, or utilized in a group of caregivers who take turns reflecting in some depth with a consultant on a particular visit. Following a visit, the caregiver can read through the list of religious themes and discern what, if any were present, explicit or implicit, in the conversation. The caregiver can recall, as much as possible, what response was made to those themes and brainstorm two or three additional responses that might have explored the theme a little further. With a consultant, or in a group, caregivers can roleplay focusing and extending dialogue in this way to address an area for growth or to affirm practice of faith, gaining further experience in pastoral conversation. Familiarity with a range of theological themes enhances the caregiver's ability to hear an extraordinary "version" in an ordinary story, provided this practice does not dismiss the person's own interpretation.

Assessment by pastoral caregivers has often been implicit or intuitive, based on traditional pastoral actions, categories of psychological assessment and common emphases in pastoral care on being "present with," or being empathic (Fitchett, 1993). A more holistic model aids caregivers in listening for and gathering pertinent information about a person's medical status, psychological state, family system, psychosocial factors, ethnic and cultural background, and societal factors. Assessment in visitation includes observing and listening for the psychosocial aspects of the person's life and circumstances: class, finances, important activities, neighborhood, housing, interests, hobbies, education, employment, and developmental perspective.

Ethnic and cultural background can be noted in visits in order to appreciate people in their context and "to avoid inappropriately imposing values" from one's own culture. Caregivers listen for and interpret the ways in which cultural forces and societal issues may contribute to suffering so that we do not hold an individual accountable for what is primarily a social or cultural problem. This discernment includes understanding differences between the caregiver and the person being visited in terms of power and dominance based on race or gender. Increasing awareness of these differences enables a caregiver to monitor presumptions of authority or lack of assertion, which may result.

Caregivers organize the information they hear according to the purpose of their visits and a list of theological or religious themes and holistic dimensions of the person and situation can draw attention to areas that are important but often overlooked. Caregivers can become aware of their biases and tendencies to distort information by using such lists for reflection following visits. When we have in mind these broad dimensions of a person's life and circumstances, our listening expands and we can hear a good deal of information in a relatively brief encounter. Caregivers can be intentional in asking about missing pieces of information, especially those areas they have a tendency to ignore, in order to compensate for known personal limits.

Pastoral assessment in its simplest form, within the context of a caregiving visit, involves answering two questions: what is going on, and what, if anything is needed? In the vignette of Sally and Melissa, a lot has already gone on. The pastor is opening space in which pastoral care may occur, showing regard for the integrity of the treatment program and after-care plan, but wanting to offer care specific to Melissa's relationship with her as pastor. Because Melissa is a teenager, Sally would need to address the issue of confidentiality with Melissa and her parents so that everyone is clear about information sharing. One option is to meet occasionally with Melissa and her parents in order to facilitate their conversation with one another, if needed. While the situation certainly involves a problem, and in that way is more problem-focused than most of this discussion of visitation, it illustrates how a pastor uses a visit for purposes of care alongside, or in congruence with, a broader spectrum of help already occurring.

If Melissa's situation included specific limiting psychosocial aspects, such as dropping out of a school where she had been threatened and no longer felt safe, or if part-time employment to help with family expenses was leading to exhaustion, then such information could make a big difference in the care Sally offers. Sally could have listened to Melissa with Pruyser and Oates's "pattern of spiritual inquiry," and wondered with her about her sense of God's providence and care or her feelings of being fated and unable to pursue her dreams. Sally could have explored the times when discouragement, fear, and anxiety over-take Melissa, when and how her faith and courage push back such discouragement.

Sally might have had biblical and theological themes in mind, such as confession and repentance and could have spoken with Melissa about her sense of getting on a different track, what she is turning away from, what she is moving toward, and how God's grace encourages her on this different path. Or it could be that Sally would hear how Melissa has been coerced by peers and needs to be supported in claiming her freedom and agency, or her identity as a child of God, and in so doing to resist harmful influence. Closing their conversation with prayer would also interpret Melissa's experience and present hope in the wider grace of God. Further, if Sally or any of the individuals in this situation identified a pattern of need among Melissa's peer group or at her school, these aspects too can become "pastoral assessment" of a wider need, shaping goals for ministry in the community based on pastoral care.

ETHICAL CONDUCT

The following brief comments concern confidentiality and records about visits, practicing within the limits of one's competence, physical contact in visitation, self-care, and safety. I mention adequate self-care for caregivers because its absence is thought to be one of the primary contributing factors in sexual misconduct among pastors. A great deal of material is now available concerning ethical behavior, personal boundaries, and sexual misconduct as a violation of sacred trust in a pastoral relationship (Doehring, 1995; Fortune, 1989; Fortune and Poling, 1994; Houts, 1991; Miles, 1999; Miller and Jackson, 1995, 23–41; Poling, 1991). While this section does not fully cover ethical conduct for caregivers, it does call attention to some crucial components for visitation.

Confidentiality

A pastor can set the standard for confidentiality early in a relationship with a congregation by communicating publicly what it means (Liberman and Woodruff, 1993; Miller and Jackson, 1995). For instance, a note in the church newsletter or a few sentences in a pastoral letter can express openness to conversation with members, and an understanding that personal information shared will be held in confidence in order to respect and protect that person. The limitation of confidentiality is reached with their permission or to protect their well-being, as when harm to self or another appears to be imminent. Knowledge of physical abuse of a child or older person unable to act on their own behalf are also situations in which caregivers are obligated to communicate information to persons qualified to intervene. If a group of lay caregivers is planning to meet as a peer consultation or support group, and intends to share information from visits, this intention too needs to be communicated clearly and in advance as part of the visitation program. Again, the purpose is not to preclude a peer group for caregivers, but if discussion of the content of their visits is going to occur, the members of the congregation need to be informed of this practice.

Records

Some notation of visits is necessary, but extensive notetaking is not warranted for pastoral visits. For some programs, the simple system of a 3 by 5 card on which the person's name, address, family members, and phone number is listed is sufficient space for noting the date visited and a sentence or two describing the content of the visit, and any follow-up to be made. Such a small card system is quite useful in the caregivers' ongoing prayers for members of the church, making it easy to choose a short list of persons for particular attention in prayer that week, for instance. Other caregivers may want or need more information—such as the length of time the person has been a member; the activities in which the person has been involved at the church; perhaps a recent time and talent inventory; some brief history of major events, such as birth of a child, death of a loved one, serious illness, or the like—may be desirable.

Sexual Misconduct

Pastors should be familiar with the definition of ethical behavior, misconduct, and sexual harassment in their denomination's policies. These definitions are also helpful in alerting lay caregivers about the importance of personal boundaries and unwelcome or inappropriate touching, and knowing that the recipient and not the caregiver defines these behaviors. For this reason, the rule-of-thumb for caregivers recommends caution in *initiating* touch with the exception of a handshake in a cultural context that considers it an appropriate greeting initiated by men or women. Any sexual contact or ambiguous "sexualized" touch or talk initiated by a caregiver or the person they visit violates this relationship of trust. Although many caregivers would prefer the freedom to express warmth by initiating a hug, many other things communicate warmth and regard and are less likely to be intrusive in a few situations, and are therefore the rule-of-thumb for all. Good eye contact, warm tone of voice, accurate empathy that communicates understanding, body posture sufficiently close in proximity but not too close, respecting the other person's sense of personal space—these are effective means of communicating warmth and regard across a wide variety of ministry contexts.

Because caregivers may be attributed power and authority by those whom they visit, caregivers need to assume that it is uncomfortable for a person to refuse a hug offered by a caregiver, or even to end a prolonged handshake. Some people don't have sufficient experience or are so accustomed to boundary violations that they are unable to define what is appropriate behavior. They trust that a caregiver's pattern of behavior establishes this definition. If the person visited initiates contact, the caregiver certainly does not need to refuse the contact, but it is the responsibility of the caregiver to discern an appropriate response, to move away or move back when a hug or physical proximity is too close and too long. It is still the immediate and much later perception of the person visited which defines what is appropriate, even if that contact was at their initiative.

Self-Care and Personal Safety

Care of caregivers represents a vital subject that is more important than these brief comments indicate. Keeping perspective about the pace and "place" of a caregiver's efforts in relation to what God is doing means having adequate balance between patience and action. Caregivers cannot sustain the type of visitation described here without consistent personal and corporate worship experiences and regular opportunities for nurture and replenishment of body and soul. The need for consultation and/or a peer support group of caregivers with whom one meets on a regular basis is a crucial aspect of self-care in order to avoid the hazard of isolation to which many in pastoral ministry are prone (Rassieur, 1991). Continued opportunities for learning and growth in caregiving help to sustain motivation for visitation and improve effectiveness in ministry. Finding healthy and faithful ways to attend to one's emotional and physical needs for intimacy apart from offering care is a key factor in self-care and in preventing inappropriate and unethical behavior.

Personal safety is a concern in any program of visitation and caution must be exercised, particularly if the caregiver is not familiar with the neighborhood, needs to ask for directions, or must walk on the street for any distance. Depending on the known risk to personal safety, teams of two caregivers may be the reasonable way to manage this risk. Parishioners who live in the area to be visited will be helpful in discerning what is best. Safety can be an issue within the home of a member or friend as well, and again reasonable caution should be used. If the person to be visited is not known by anyone currently in the congregation, a caregiver team of two should go to see the person on a first visit as a reasonable precaution.

The particular needs of a local church shape the ongoing process of equipping caregivers. Many caregivers find that practicing listening skills in roleplays result in improved relationships with family and friends. Being well equipped as a caregiver can infiltrate other areas of one's life in the most desirable ways. The final chapter focuses on planning a program of visitation, illustrations of programs that include visitation, guidelines for a specific visit, and the conclusion.

Steps to Action

1. With a partner, or as a group of caregivers if possible, take turns engaging in a roleplay in which the person designated as caregiver uses only simple repetition responses five times in a row (a surprisingly difficult assignment). Videotape the roleplay, if at all possible, and play back for evaluation. The person in the careseeker role may portray a simple personal problem provided it is resolved, or discuss a current practice of faith in which further growth is sought. The purpose of the roleplay is to practice listening skills, not to stump the caregiver, so avoid portraying complex, multiple-issue types of situations.

2. Partners in the roleplay evaluate the interaction and pause the tape at each point after the caregiver has responded; if no video is used, evaluate the roleplay as a whole. Comment on how it felt to be in the caregiver and careseeker roles at that point in the dialogue. Evaluate whether the caregiver's responses were simple repetitions and if so, how accurate they were to the careseeker's statement. Brainstorm alternative simple repetition responses that could have been used.

3. Partners enact a second roleplay in which some partial rephrasing occurs in a five-minute interaction (this exercise should be easier than the first roleplay), and follow the same evaluation process.

4. Partners then engage in a third five-minute roleplay using one or two whole paraphrase responses, and follow the evaluation process.

5. In a final roleplay, at least fifteen minutes in length, partners engage in dialogue with the careseeker, demonstrating a mixture of all three levels of reflection.

6. In a separate peer group consultation meeting, or additional caregiver training session, use the final, longer roleplay if it has been videotaped, or enact another, and discuss these questions as partners, or as a group:

a) What, if anything, is troubling the person? If the interaction focused primarily on growth, what specifically will be different when this growth is achieved? How do the three domains of experience—affect, behavior, and cognition—interact and conflict in the problem or in the desired growth?

b) If the dialogue is problem-focused, what is causing the problem? If the interaction is focused on growth, what has prevented such growth thus far? Briefly identify "types" of causes for the problem or impediment to growth, not only where it began, but what keeps it going.

c) Evaluate the careseeker's situation asking what was missing or deficient, especially in the areas of work (doing), relationships (moving toward or away from others), and aloneness (attending to, but not preoccupied with internal reality). After gathering these comments, hear evaluation of what was missing for the careseeker from both people who were in the roleplay.

d) Brainstorm how the roleplay might have concluded, had it been a full visit with someone, and whether an appropriate goal would likely have been change, choice, or confusion reduction. How might the caregiver have explored what was needed in addressing the problem or encouraging desired growth? Hear from the people who played the roles.

7. If time allows, or in a subsequent session, evaluate the roleplay for themes, images, actions, or strong feelings expressed by the careseeker. Listening "into" the dialogue, identify what biblical or theological themes are explicitly stated or "echoed," evaluate whether they were explored, and gather ideas for how this portion of the interaction could have been strengthened. Briefly enact one or two of these ideas, picking up the roleplay at the point where a different tack might have been taken, and discuss whether it was effective.

8. Roleplay should continue as part of every peer consultation meeting for caregivers, or be included in individual work with a consultant. The format of practicing basic listening skills and intentionally listening "into" an interchange for biblical or theological themes should be included on a regular basis.

9. The leader or facilitator for a caregivers group should ask at every peer group meeting if an issue of ethical conduct has been encountered in the past month. Create an environment in which discussion of confidentiality, keeping notes, maintaining appropriate personal boundaries, self-care, and personal safety are a part of every meeting so that ethical conduct is supported, rather than waiting for a problem to arise.

10. Caregivers can reflect on visits they have made individually, with another caregiver, or as a group. Pastoral assessment should be a key element in this reflection, to assure accurate identification of problem areas, desire for growth, or simple affirmation of faithfulness.

Identify the dimensions in the person's life and circumstances that influence resolution of the problem or readiness for further growth. Review the psychosocial factors in Fitchett's model, and the summary of Pruyser and Oates's religious themes to broaden perspective. Caregivers may not need to reflect at length on *every* visit they make, but to do so quite thoroughly with at least one visit each month will continue to enhance effectiveness in ministry.

5

OFFERING CARE—
AN ACTION PLAN

A number of years ago Alfred Krass initiated a program of spiritual direction in his congregation (1987). Often identified as a "social action minister," he became dismayed at how few parishioners were participating in individual or group disciplines of Bible study and prayer. He described his visit to a physician for an annual checkup and the paperwork he filled out while waiting for the appointment. He listed his allergies and family history, and was gratified to respond to a question about regular exercise.

> But then [the doctor] asked, "Do you take an annual vacation?" and "Do you take a day off every week?" This was certainly a unique doctor! He went on to ask about time spent with spouse and/or family. The final question was: "Do you spend daily or weekly time in prayer or meditation?" That one blew my mind. . . . If a medical doctor is aware that sabbath rest, prayer and meditation are good for patients' health, and if he doesn't hesitate to ask them whether they are following such practices, why am I, a pastor—professionally involved in what used to be called "the cure of souls"—so reluctant to ask such questions? (Krass, 1987, 311)

Indeed, the pastor wondered why clergy do not expect parishioners to come to them for regular "spiritual checkups!" Acknowledging that this practice would go against what our society regards as "private," the pastor chose to move forward, to exercise pastoral leadership by assisting every member in having an annual spiritual checkup. He devised an inventory for people to complete, a checkup that was basically a self-examination, based on Paul's prayer for the well-being of the Christians at Colossae found in Colossians 1:9-14. He then arranged half-hour interviews to go through the questionnaire with each member, and publicized his availability as a spiritual friend or counselor.

Several things struck me about this pastor's program for exploring "signs of health" or wellness and his desire to "open their eyes to a new vision of what in Christ we could become" (Krass, 312). First, his initiative and exercise of pastoral leadership and authority exemplify the best in what shepherding means in pastoral care. Second, his program used power and authority with respect for people's privacy, and clarified that *he* was not checking up on *them*. He was inviting conversation about their own spiritual self-examination, and trusting that it would contribute to the spiritual health of individuals and the congregation.

The type of visitation in this illustration reflects God's initiative in extending grace to us, and it demonstrates a particular type of relationship between pastor and parishioner. The type of authority "borrowed" from the physician supports and encourages inquiry about another's life of faith; at the same time, it is not a coercive or demanding authority but an exercise of leadership that admits pastoral limits and respects personal boundaries.

As pastoral leader I am one traveler on pilgrimage speaking to and caring for other pilgrims. I can be a spiritual friend and, if they wish, a mentor or guide. But I dare not let the limitations of pluralism—limitations I respect—keep me from exercising the pastoral role that God wants congregational leaders to exercise. That's different from asking the members to accompany me on my journey. But it's also different from the despairing attitude that says pastoring belongs to a past era. Ultimately we will all answer to God and not to one another, but along the way the Divine Pastor gifts the congregation with pastors who assist us in being accountable for our discipleship. I am trying to find a way to be such a helper (Krass, 1987, 312).

Exercising pastoral leadership in this way requires the desire and capacity to function as helper and guide while respecting another's difference, integrity, and freedom.

A second illustration of a comprehensive visitation program integrated fully into a broader congregational program was called a "Membership Reaffirmation Process." A good intention to move toward visitation of all the membership of the congregation was initially thwarted by inaccurate member records. As it happened, the church staff was moving to computerized member information software, requiring different management of this data. A larger congregation-wide program was launched out of practical obstacles. Lay caregivers aided in the difficult process of tracking down correct information, and the church's governing body took initiative to contact members who were known to be inactive. But the theme that was carried through several church school classes, sermons, stewardship campaign, and liturgical seasons was the meaning of membership, literally regathering the congregation's activities as people committed to following Jesus Christ in new ways. The visitation program was launched in the fall and concluded at Pentecost of the following year, with a special litany of reaffirmation and offering of commitments to love and serve God at the Pentecost worship service.

Such a thematic approach makes it easier for lay caregivers to interpret the rationale for comprehensive visiting if it is a concern. It also offers the opportunity for an inventory or questionnaire of sorts as a basis for pastoral conversation. Many congregations prefer a time and talents inventory, often used on an annual basis in connection with a stewardship theme or time of special commitment (see note 10 at the end of the text). Such an inventory could be modified to include brief stories about efforts in reconciliation, conflict resolution, or community building in one's place of work. Space could be provided for other volunteer activities in the community, interpreted as extending the pastoral care of the congregation into the wider community. Notation of an ongoing ministry of prayer should always be included in such an inventory, as almost everyone is able to participate.

Another approach to visitation is a "covenanting process" in pastoral home visits as suggested by Suzanne Coyle (1985). The purpose of the visits is a "covenanting" process between member and church, represented by the pastor. Coyle draws upon biblical, theological, and psychological understanding of covenant to describe a process in which the pastor mediates between the member or family and the congregation, stating and renegotiating expectations and hopes for the future. Active members who do not appear to be having a problem are included to confirm that a covenant relationship changes, grows, and needs to be reassessed and renegotiated from time to time in response to life circumstances, not just in response to crises.

Coyle reclaims the home visit as the preferred setting for this covenanting process and identifies four stages in the process. The first step is building a foundation for discussion of the covenant relation between member and congregation, and the second is clarifying the member's existing expectations of the covenant—what they expect to give to and receive from the church. The third step is renegotiating the contract, including discussion of personal faith (and whether the church helps with this), expression of feelings, and concrete steps to be taken in mending broken relationships with other members, the pastor, or with God. The final step is the expression of new expectations and resolution as a result of experiencing a caring relationship with the pastor. Coyle states, "One key purpose of a covenanting process in the home visit is to make assumptions explicit and to move into a constructive and intentional relationship between God, the church, church member and pastor" (1985, 109).

A fourth illustration of pastoral visitation occurred in the context of a specialized ministry. In this example, an ecumenical cluster of congregations received funding for a pilot project in single-parent ministry. The pastoral staff person for initiating this ministry used information about single parents who had received assistance through the food and clothing bank located in one of the churches. Contact was made through a letter and phone call (to those who had phones), as well as by word of mouth among several of the women who were friends. Home visits were made when possible, and in-office visits at the church when necessary, to meet and talk with each single parent in order to design a ministry responsive to their needs.

As the ministry developed, it included small peer group meetings for the women, occasional retreats for the women and their children, and advocacy by the pastoral staff and the women themselves with local police and social service agencies to address concerns for safety, education, and employment. As more single parents participated in the program, caregivers were recruited from the congregations in the cluster as mentor/partners for the parents, some of whom became members of the congregations themselves.

In each of these illustrations, pastoral visitation played a key role in fostering faithfulness among the members and in the congregation, and in some cases, in the wider community.

PLANNING PROCESS

Taking the initiative in pastoral visitation means moving toward other people and entering into their world. For this reason alone, many caregivers do not act on good intentions, though they may respond well enough to crisis situations and obvious needs for visiting those hospitalized or bereaved. But more systematic visitation of all members and friends of a congregation requires initiative and motivation, shaped by the particular size, type, and needs of the congregation. For some pastors, due to the size of the congregation or their interpretation of pastoral care, it is important to carry this responsibility alone and they are able to do so quite well. Many pastors find that sharing this responsibility with lay caregivers is in itself motivating, but face difficulties in recruiting, training, and maintaining a group of caregivers in their congregation.

Other pastors in a multiple staff church designate a particular staff member for pastoral care and visit only on an "as needed" basis. And still others will always prefer to visit spontaneously, without planning and perhaps without much preparation. On occasion such visits may be quite "inspired" and effective, but most caregivers, myself included, are limited enough in perspective that we need more intentional thought about who's missing and who we are ignoring. Further, the major point of a more intentional approach is to engage in pastoral conversation with those who have relative "well-being" as well as persons more overtly in need. I trust that the Spirit is able to work through both intentional and spontaneous visits, but that the intentional compensates more for our limits as caregivers.

Caregivers reading this book may be considering moving from intention to action, or altering a visitation program already in place. They may be faced with a recognized discrepancy between the visiting-that-is and the visiting-that-could-be, and so they are ready to make a choice or prepared to implement change. Moving from intention to action often involves seeking information about the problem, anticipating obstacles or challenges to resolving it, and seeing some of the advantages of making the desired change (Miller and Jackson, 1995, 114–27). One professor/mentor who helped me along the way often suggested I try a new approach or difficult task as an experiment before deciding whether to move forward with it in a fuller way. If being "comprehensive" sounds like an obstacle, or if the notion of a "program" is too big a commitment, then by all means set those ideas aside for now. Proceed, instead, with a time-limited "experiment" approach, learning from what works and what doesn't work, evaluating and making adjustments as you go along. Planning visits with members better known to the caregiver as primarily supportive, for instance, helps to enhance and maintain motivation for pastoral visits. Such a nonheroic approach to visiting is preferred if it helps to sustain an effective process of caregiving in the long run.

In addition to sustaining motivation for more effective visiting, several decisions occur in a planning process, as described in the following steps.

Preliminary Decisions

Discern the level of motivation or readiness for such a program, acknowledging roadblocks in moving from intention to action, and identifying what information or action would enhance the caregivers' motivation. Talk with pastoral colleagues who have visitation programs in place to hear from others' experience.

Discuss the idea with appropriate church staff and leadership personnel, and committees concerned with staff time usage, pastoral care, mission outreach, and so on as needed for broad based input. Arrive at a preliminary decision as democratically as possible.

Purpose Statement

Identify the purpose of the visits as relationship building, fostering faithfulness, enhancing connections among members, congregation, and community, as appropriate for the congregation. Framing visitation in relation to another program of the church may shape the purpose more clearly for members if they are accustomed to special needs visits only. This decision needs to be made with the leadership of the congregation and through prayerful consideration about the life of the faith community.

Decide who will be visited: active and inactive members, friends of the congregation, prospective members, and others, depending on the congregation's self-understanding. The program as described here would be in addition to regular visits to the hospital, care center, and in crisis situations, and would be displaced by these needs from time to time. Visits in the community could include persons asking for assistance at the church, sites of outreach efforts with other churches and synagogues, social service agencies, homeless shelters, health care centers, university dorms or campus ministries, or apartment buildings in the neighborhood, depending on the nature of the congregation and its sense of boundaries and connections. Discerning patterns of need through visiting may point in the direction of other kinds of visits, contacts, and connections that need to be made or strengthened.

The purpose for the visits and who will be visited can be stated in a preliminary manner at this point, pending other steps in the process. Have in mind a tentative date for beginning the program, especially if it is tied to the church year or will begin in the fall in connection with other church programs.

Prospective Caregivers

Decide who will be doing the visits, the involvement of pastoral staff persons, and possible recruitment of lay caregivers shaped by the congregation's size, needs, staff, and the purpose of the visits. Identify the availability of staff persons (daytime, evening, weekends) and realistic frequency for visits (in addition to hospital, care center, or crisis visits). Many pastors may realistically do two home visits per week; other caregivers choose to visit every member/family once a year.

Experimenting for a month or two may help determine what is realistic for existing staff. Set a pace that can be consistently maintained.

If lay caregivers will be recruited in order to accomplish the purpose of the visits, the number of visits to be made, or the frequency within a given period, an existing pastoral care type of committee may become involved. Consider the number of persons needed as caregivers and the members of the congregation who may be ready for this commitment. I do not recommend asking for volunteers for caregiving, and encourage individual face-to-face invitation (preferably in the home!) to consider participating in this ministry. At this point, a preliminary list of potential caregivers can be prepared.

Consider what additional training or support may be needed for a pastor alone or for a group of caregivers who will visit. Gather ideas for an initial training process for a group of caregivers, and estimate the cost, if any. Stephen Ministries, a structured training program for visitation, is an option if a church is prepared to make that commitment (see footnote 10 at the end of the book). Some may prefer to experiment and move forward with visiting for a time before making a large commitment. Explore options for ongoing consultation for pastor and/or other caregivers and obtain accurate information about the estimated cost on an annual basis.

Unintended Consequences

Assess and prepare for the impact of the program on pastoral and support staff, both initial preparation and ongoing administration and maintenance. Identify estimated expenses and if, when, and how all or part could be budgeted. If use of facilities for training or peer group meetings of caregivers is a concern, note this effect.

Obtain accurate information about members and friends of the congregation including up-to-date address, phone number, employment hours, if known, family members, and persons living in the home.

Predict difficulties or roadblocks, impact on other informal caregiving networks in the congregation, and expect times of discouragement for a caregiver. Build in experiences of support and encouragement through regular, monthly consultation or peer group meetings. Expect that personal needs or other commitments will overtake caregivers from time to time.

Revise purpose, persons to be visited, number or type of potential caregivers, staff, budget, training needs, and start date after all these factors have been assessed in a tentative manner. Proceed on a time-limited, experimental basis, if needed, and reassess the effect on factors least known in order to make further adjustments.

Launching Visitation

Decide when to begin. Seasonal or programmatic emphases may answer this question. Consider some form of commissioning in worship, if appropriate, or other public acknowledgment of the caregivers or "launching" of a program.

Recruit lay caregivers, clarifying what they're being asked to do, time involved, risk factors, and what training and support will be available.

Prepare a referral resources list, if not already available.

Publicize the purpose of the visits in the newsletter and announce it in worship, including preferred location, whether a meal is expected, and approximate length of visits.

Recommended location for the visits is in homes, but this is not required. Other acceptable options such as a coffee shop or the pastor's study may be used. Caregivers need to visit in teams if the neighborhood is not known by the visitor or is unsafe.

Offer a training workshop or series of workshops for a group of caregivers, depending on need. Secure and distribute good up-to-date street or road maps for caregivers of the areas to be visited.

Distribute or assign visits with "matching" as needed if a group of caregivers is used, and plan a gathering after the first visit or two are completed. Assigning teams is an option.

Establish individual caregiver follow-up to particular visits and peer support group meetings once a month. Engage in pastoral theological reflection and prayer regarding the visits made.

Evaluate the program, and experiment, adjust, or try something different if a problem arises. Assess ongoing training needs.

Provide graceful conclusion for caregivers who need to end their work by their own choice or due to review of their efforts.

VISITATION GUIDELINES

The following guidelines address practical concerns in visiting:

1. Review information about the person or family available from church records, phone, address, directions to the home or meeting place. Decide whether to make the visit alone or as a team of two lay caregivers.

2. Phone in advance and begin by restating the purpose of the visit, who would be visiting, preference for a home visit, and any request for particular family members to be present. Provided that the visitation program and its purpose have been publicized in advance, it is better not to ask "if" they "want" a visit, but to ask when would be a convenient time. Arrange a specific time for the visit, based on the caregiver's prior decision about available times and the needs of the person or family being visited. In most instances, no visit should be scheduled for later than 8 P.M., or 7 P.M. if there are young children.

If a visit is refused you may ask if there is anything you need to know that would help the congregation in extending care to the person in some other way. If no further thoughts or feelings are shared, then the caregiver may follow up the next time the person is encountered at the church, with a simple warm greeting. If the person does not participate in the congregation, the pastor and lay caregiving group will need to decide how to continue to extend care.

3. Preparing for the scheduled visit involves prayer, with the assumption that God is present and at work in the person's life, in their family or network of friends, in the congregation, and in the wider community. I suggest praying for the person, including each family member by name and their respective efforts to love and serve God through these connections. Reflect on the person's life in this web of interrelations, to the extent you are aware of them, and note any strong connections that you could encourage or any "missing" links about which you could inquire. The assumption is not that more is better, but a kind of preliminary assessment of the person, for those who are doing relatively well and for those with more evident problems. Reflect on previous visits or recent contacts with the person and their current work situation, commitment to and responsibility for friends or family members, involvement in church activities, or volunteer work in the community. Prayer before visiting also focuses the caregiver as a potential instrument in the context of what God is already doing or calling forth in a particular situation, as God chooses. A caregiver is initiating interaction, but a nonheroic approach is best, recognizing that other people and processes are effectively fostering faithfulness as well. Reflection and prayer before a visit may also bring to mind a particular passage of scripture.

4. The caregiver will need a Bible and perhaps a liturgical resource and communion kit if communion is to be shared. After reflection upon family members in their context, and prayer for each person by name, most caregivers will be ready to recollect names when the visit occurs. If remembering names is a problem, write them down and review the names several times on the way to their home.

5. Practical considerations when entering another person's home include arriving on time, accepting but not expecting hospitality. If the television is on and distracting, but a family member appears to be engaged in watching rather than visiting, the caregiver may state a preference that it be turned off, but requesting that it be turned down may be a reasonable compromise. If no introductions are provided and the caregiver does not know everyone present, initiate self-introduction. Ask where the person would like you to be seated, in close enough

proximity to those whose hearing is known to be impaired. A caregiver's urgent needs for food, a drink, a bathroom, or a phone should be met before entering the home. Caregivers introduce themselves to anyone present whom they haven't met, including children, and I recommend shaking hands rather than hugging. If you can smell the coffee brewing when you walk in, accept the hospitality someone has taken time to prepare. Reiterate the purpose of the visit, as publicized in advance: an opportunity to get to know one another better, part of our program for assuring folks feel connected, a step in reflecting more on what it means to be faithful, gathering the member's thoughts and feelings about how we can more effectively work on some of the problems in our neighborhood, or some more immediate and obvious concern that particular day.

Caregivers need to offer some sense of the length of time they have in mind, even if it was mentioned earlier in the phone call to schedule the visit. For instance: "I'd hoped we could talk about you and what's going on in your journey for thirty minutes or so; how does that sound to you?" "As you know, I'm here to learn a little more about your Lenten reflections, and what part of the daily Bible study has been most important to you so far. If we could end by 8:00 that would be helpful to me." "I'd like to take about forty minutes with you, if I may, to understand more of how you're learning and growing in discipleship. You've read about that in the church newsletter, right?" Framing the visit in purpose and time is part of the structuring task of the caregiver so that everyone knows what to expect and can make judgments about what they want to share on that basis. It also helps people make decisions about whether to go ahead and put children to bed, or to signal to you that Rachel needs to get to soccer practice, so we'll need to leave at 4:15. The caregiver can then plan accordingly.

Questions that inquire about thoughts, feelings, and behaviors can be used to invite people to expand and elaborate on a particular point, or to clarify any confusion or vagueness in what is being said: What are your thoughts about [a faith practice that's important to you]? What is your feeling about [the meaning of your membership]? What are you already doing that comes closest to [desired change]? What have you done that is close to [desired growth]? A mistake often made by inexperienced caregivers is asking too many information questions: When did that happen? Who was there with you? Where were you at the time? and so on. Gathering this factual type of information gives caregivers something to say, but is not especially helpful in facilitating pastoral conversation.

Inviting people to consider their experience in terms of interconnections with the congregation, local community, and culture factors that seem to be at work can be a crucial part of discerning what, if anything needs to change. For instance, Henry might have asked Al about the congregation's care for persons unable to attend worship and what Al would suggest to enhance these connections. The pastor visiting Marie could inquire what role the pastor or congregation might have in advocating for necessary repairs and improved housing, or offer to facilitate communication with the local school board to address children's safety to and from school.

Caregivers can identify desired change, options, and goals for personal or congregational action or response, and identify implications for broader social action and change to be addressed through political action (Graham, 1992; Neuger, 1996). Caregivers can listen to personal stories with a view toward social systems and cultural context and make these broader connections to an individual's experience (Gunderson, 1997; Graham, 1992; Gerkin, 1991). When the pastor visited Melissa and heard her intentions to overcome substance abuse, the pastor's acknowledgment of the pressure of a peer group and identification of the popular cultural mediums (favorite TV shows, movies, or current fashions romanticizing substance abuse) that reinforce the problem act to support Melissa's efforts. Inviting Melissa to clarify the unintended consequences of such popular portrayals (addictive patterns of behavior, alienation in relationships, damage to emotional and physical health, increased vulnerability to violence) in her own experience may strengthen and encourage her ability to make different choices. Further, the relationship with a caregiver serves to contradict perpetuating causes of harm to self through firm and gentle affirmation of Melissa's renewed hopes for her future.

The pastor who had lunch with Jim at the club listens as Jim explains what he would like to see happen at the church. Jim also talks about his current efforts on behalf of a political candidate and his strong convictions in support of the party's platform. The pastor acknowledges a difference in their views on the subject, of which Jim was already aware, but goes on to invite Jim to share more about how these political views are connected to his faith, his sense of vocation, and his mature self-understanding as citizen and church leader.

Concluding a visit means signaling in advance that the identified time frame is closing. Caregivers need to summarize, briefly, what they have heard, perhaps in terms of what they have learned in the course of conversation. They may ask for feedback, whether a visit has been helpful, or what has been most and least helpful. It is important to identify clearly what, if any follow-up will occur by the caregiver and those visited. Plans for future visits should be noted. Collective prayer either with all participating or at least gathered thoughts from those present is often an effective closure of a visit.

When it is unclear whether a person acknowledges the pastoral "role" of the caregiver, or ambivalence about this role is evident, a more open question is "Would you like me to pray with you now, or to remember you in my own prayers later?" It may be that reference to or reading of scripture has been a part of the pastoral conversation. During some visits no reference to scripture is made, and no passage read, and a caregiver should not feel obligated to "tack on" such reading. Doing so may actually diminish regard for the Bible and imply that God's living Word is not already a part of the conversation. Concluding the visit within the time frame noted at the beginning of the conversation shows respect for all present. It is the caregiver's responsibility to structure the visit. It is quite acceptable for caregivers to look at a clock on the wall or their own wristwatch in order to signal closure to the visit. This visual cue is particularly effective if it occurs about ten minutes before a visit is to conclude, giving people an opportunity to discuss matters that have not been addressed.

Following a visit, a process of pastoral theological reflection occurs. Notes may be made for information that needs to be given to other staff members (correcting names, ages, persons now living in the home, current interests, plans to move, or other "public" information). Confidential information may be noted briefly as discussed earlier in this chapter. Follow-up may include networking with other committees in the church or with a community agency if the caregiver has committed to securing information for the person visited. Notes about patterns of need discerned on an ongoing basis may be made for discussion with the pastor or caregivers peer group. Eventually such patterns of need can be addressed programmatically through the church, through an ecumenical effort in the community, or through advocacy with a social service agency or local government organization. Caregivers should discuss these needs with the pastor and appropriate leadership in the church before speaking on behalf of the congregation in order to decide the most adequate response. Alleviation and prevention of suffering among those visited and in the wider community is one way in which pastoral care becomes an effective form of "public" ministry.

Pastoral theological reflection may occur alone, in individual consultation, or in a caregivers group, and is crucial for sustaining ongoing visitation. The first step in this reflection process is to identify one's feelings, whether they informed the care offered, or were appropriately set aside. Second, assess the integrity and effectiveness of the caregiver, perhaps reflecting on the three metaphors for caregivers. Third, consider whether the parables of the kingdom resonate with your sense of this visit, and "wonder" what God is doing or calling forth in the person visited, in your own life, and in the community of faith, as a result of this visit. Fourth, evaluate the skills utilized during the visit, identifying areas of strength and those needing improvement, and note concerns for ongoing training. Fifth, decide whether a need exists for additional consultation, discussion in a caregiver peer group, or referral for other skilled help. Sixth, reflect on the connections or links with the local and wider community, which were named in this visit, and any patterns of need in the congregation or community, which may be appearing.

ENCOURAGING CONNECTIONS

Pastoral visitation is one of the things I love the most about serving in a local church, close encounters of a different sort than I now experience teaching students in a divinity school, and working with clients in the school's pastoral counseling center. I remember feeling nurtured as a pastor, sitting in the backyard sipping lemonade, listening to the well-seasoned parishioner I wanted to be like when I "grew up." I remember cake fresh out of the oven and tea carefully prepared, and the gentle reception I experienced in so many homes, hospitality extended in a manner I so admire and rarely emulate.

I do also remember the unpleasant and difficult visits, when the street was on the map, but refused to appear as I drove around and around with inadequate directions, and the frustration of trying to contact inactive members who didn't attend worship and didn't have phones. I remember the adult daughter who opposed "organized religion," and left the room after she found out I was her mother's pastor, and the visit with a member whose husband kept calling me "honey." I recollect too well the visit at a church officer's home, sweat beading on my forehead as he got "in my face" in his kitchen, pointing his finger at me, angry about the committee on which he was asked to serve.

I recall, too, the endurance of the church member with whom conversation was possible only as she labored to type each letter, one by one on her home computer, her speech impaired so that I could not understand most of her words when she spoke. And the courage of the man who was himself a lay caregiver in the congregation, bowed on the floor of his living room, struggling to breath as his throat constricted with progressive disease. These experiences have been formative for my personal efforts in faithfulness in ways I don't altogether understand, but I view these encounters as gifts along the way in my own process of making meaning, losing my way, and trying again. Pastoral visitation is an opportunity for touching and being touched by the lives of others, which does not occur unless caregivers make the time, go to see, and enter the intimate space of another. (Occasionally, recalling the spilled buckets of feed for the sheep, it is painful and humiliating, and you pick yourself up, head for the truck, and go ask for help.)

Taking the initiative to understand people and their lives of faith, taking time to inquire about their practices of faith, to hear the links they are making in discipleship between the community of faith and its wider social context—this is a pastoral opportunity that requires first-hand experience and face-to-face encounter. An intentional, every-member strategy for ongoing visitation in a local church is one way in which caregivers can reflect God's gracious initiative toward all persons, encouraging the vitality of their faith and its practice as individuals and as a community.

Moving from good intentions for pastoral visitation to taking the initiative in noncrisis, nonproblem-focused visitation is worth the effort. It is difficult for anyone who leans toward the efficient use of time and energy based on time management principles. The type of pastoral visitation I am recommending even may appear to fly in the face of effective leadership skills. But I believe that it moves toward preventive (not just responsive) forms of pastoral care and leads the way for a revaluing of caring relationship throughout a community of faith. In the Christian community, visitation is one of the ways caregivers try to show the love and justice of Jesus Christ, emphasizing interpersonal relationships as central to our faith, and enhancing the vital connections of congregations in and for the world.

The purpose of every-member visitation must be stated clearly and publicly in terms of relationship building and fostering practices of faith. Demonstrating interest in each and every member as a person of faith raises expectations that will likely be met by both caregivers and members. Caregivers should express interest in people and their practices of faith apart from or in addition to a particular need or difficulty or event. In a world that often limits our interactions to an impersonal exchange of goods or information, taking an interest in another and spending the time to explore even a little of how things are going in this person's life of faith is a peculiar gift of care.

Pastoral visitation may be pursued in the face of and even in resistance to other depersonalizing, dehumanizing experiences in life. Visitation can be carried out for the straightforward purpose of nurturing pastoral relationship, which fosters faith in addition to other visits with more functional purposes such as evangelism, stewardship fund-raising, or recruitment for education or other organizational tasks. The type of pastoral visitation described here values and initiates relationship for its own sake and expresses interest in people as such, not just in response to problems or particular organizational needs.

Returning to biblical images for visitation, we see that caregivers tend the soil in which the seed has been planted, join in the mix of leaven and flour that God is stirring, and accompany other guests also invited to the great dinner. God has planted the seed, added the leaven, extended the invitation, and caregivers have the opportunity to participate in a process of growth, to enter into the mix being stirred, to accompany other invited guests on the way to the feast. For caregivers, I call it fostering faithfulness.

APPENDIX

OUTLINE OF A TRAINING WORKSHOP

The following outline could be implemented in four two-hour evening sessions, or in two four-hour workshops. Material for each session may be drawn from the preceding chapters with additions from bibliographical references cited as appropriate for the particular ministry setting. Leadership for the training can be provided by the pastor, a layperson with previous training in listening skills, or an outside consultant. Each meeting should begin with a worship experience and conclude with prayer.

Session I

A. Welcome caregiver participants and initiate self-introductions based on what has led them to make this commitment to a ministry of pastoral visitation. Give an overview of what will be covered in the training process.

B. State the purpose of visitation in broader biblical, historical, and theological terms based on chapter 1. Reiterate the purpose of visitation as it has emerged in the specific congregation in which you serve. If visitation is being launched in connection with a wider church program, identify how it fits with this seasonal or thematic framework.

C. Present and discuss metaphors for caregiving based on chapter 2. Ask each participant to identify the metaphor with which they identify, and the particular strengths and hazards of this caregiving approach as it fit with their self-understanding. Invite conversation based on each participant's "growing edge," which would enable them to integrate all three approaches in caregiving, as suggested in the Steps to Action at the end of chapter 2.

D. Present material from chapter 4 listening skills on levels of reflective responses. Ask participants to engage in Steps to Action 1 and 2 as an initial task in developing skills.

Session II

A. If time has lapsed since the previous session, ask participants to identify what significant learning occurred at that time and what reflections they have had since the first session.

B. Present and discuss the metaphors for visitation based on chapter 3. Emphasize the primary theological purpose for visitation, which is supported by effective listening and helping skills.

C. Discuss visitation as an opportunity to strengthen the congregation's interconnection with the local community. State the hopes or particular goals that have been identified for this "outward" focus as members and friends are encouraged to practice their faith in the wider context.

D. Present remaining material from chapter 4 on listening skills. Follow Steps to Action 3–10 suggested at the end of chapter 4 for roleplays.

Session III

A. Present and discuss the notion of partnership and collaboration as presented in chapter 3, noting issues related to the appropriate use of power and authority.

B. Identify the current pattern of worship leadership and use of ritual forms of worship as they already occur in visits in the congregation. Discuss such leadership and what, if any change in this element of visitation is intended based on the purpose of the program.

C. Discuss pastoral conversation based on material in chapter 3. If practice of faith is the focus of the program, use the Steps to Action to roleplay and evaluate pastoral conversation, with particular attention to a collaborative rather than an intrusive approach, opening space to focus on discussion of faithfulness, and listening for theological themes.

Session IV

A. All participate in a summary of learning thus far. Identify the next step that will follow training (assignment of visits, date for next caregiver group meeting).

B. Identify elements of the planning process as discussed in chapter 4, which need to be emphasized or reiterated (frequency of visits, use of consultation, keeping notes, and the like). Give details of program implementation for the next week and month so that caregivers are clear what is expected.

C. Present information on ethical conduct and denominational policies, definitions and expectations in this program for confidentiality, self-care, and personal safety.

D. Continue roleplays of listening skills and pastoral conversation, noting that this type of practice will continue. Encourage caregivers to identify further training and growth needs that can be built into the program as it proceeds.

Conclude training with a commissioning liturgy, if possible, in the context of corporate worship (PCUSA, 1990, 1993).

NOTES

1. Going to See

1. The persons portrayed in illustrations throughout the book are composites of people encountered in ministry situations and do not represent any particular individual.

2. Fostering Faithfulness

2. One view of biblical authority and interpretation has been described as "A Divine Message in Human Thought Forms," and is characterized by: (1) openness to the insights of social science in understanding scripture, (2) paying attention to the human words, and their historical and cultural context, "neither presuming the meaning to be obvious nor forcing meaning into arbitrary harmonies or a preconceived theology," and (3) using human relational metaphors (rather than scientific, rational procedures or propositional statements) to describe God's communication with us, providing attitudes, approaches, and analogies by which we can cope with contemporary problems (United Presbyterian Church, 1982, 43–44).

3. The idea of theological assumptions implicit in acts of care and reflecting on questions to discern them was suggested by Professor Christie Neuger in a lecture at Princeton Theological Seminary in 1990. Howard Clinebell also discusses the importance of identifying "assumptive worlds" that caregivers bring to situations of ministry (1984).

4. Becoming aware of the language one regularly uses in talking about these things is one way to clarify theological assumptions. Language not only reflects an interpretation but also selectively shapes or reinforces a particular understanding and actively influences those who hear. Language regularly used around the theological assumptions may or may not be consistent with claimed beliefs about the nature of God and God's relationship with creation and humanity.

People speak of God in many ways: imminent, transcendent, omniscient, absent, judgmental, forgiving, merciful, manipulative, incarnate, father, mother, friend, justice-maker. People use language describing a theological understanding of human being as basically good, basically sinful, amenable to being changed, able to change themselves, imago dei, social, alone/isolated, penitent, saved, justified, being sanctified by God's grace.

Our lived priorities reflect assumptions about the purpose of humanity and creation: love, service, work, pleasure, justice, joy, endurance, play. Definitions of brokenness and wholeness, sin and salvation, illness and health, alienation and reconciliation are implied in our attention to physical, emotional, spiritual, interpersonal, and communal dimensions of life.

5. In this discussion, I am drawing from Donald Capp's framework, which identified the interrelation among pastoral self-understanding, praxis, "diagnostic model" or approach to a problem, and anticipated disclosure of meaning, meaning that is "larger than the immediate situation" (1984, 87). Capps' pastoral hermeneutics emphasize the "world-disclosive possibilities" in pastoral action and suggest that pastoral actions are themselves parabolic events. He identifies each of the three caregiving metaphors with particular pastoral self-understandings, the shepherd as the responsible self, the wounded healer as the believable self, and the wise fool as the accessible self (1984, 95–121).

6. For further discussion of social and political action in situations of pastoral care and counseling, see Billman, 1996, and Neuger, 1996.

7. In his study of the history of pastoral care in America, E. Brooks Holifield traces the conceptions of theology and psychology, the influence of popular culture, class structure, and the national economy on pastoral care, and the evolving organizational patterns of congregations. Holifield states,

A representative selection of pastoral conversations in the late twentieth century would probably encompass the whole history of pastoral counseling in America. Some ministers today still speak in the tightly rational accents of the seventeenth century; some still worry about eighteenth-century understandings of sin, conviction, and rebirth; some still strive for the appearance of gentility; some affect an easy and informal manner; some offer diagnoses couched in psychological jargon; some nod sympathetically and strive to reflect the right feelings. To adopt a certain style, to say some things and leave other things unsaid, is to locate oneself within a specific tradition and a specifiable history. Every pastor, wittingly or unwittingly, adopts some "theory" of pastoral counseling, whether it be derived from the seventeenth century or from the twentieth (Holifield, 1983, 349–50).

8. By "Reformed" tradition I mean the particular historical church movement that occurred in the sixteenth century in Western Europe and today affirms certain theological themes, creeds, confessions, and practices. The central theological affirmations in this tradition are the sovereignty of God and the rediscovery of God's grace in Jesus Christ as revealed in the scriptures. The Constitution of the Presbyterian Church, U.S.A., Part II Book of Order (Louisville, Ky.: Office of the General Assembly, Presbyterian Church, U.S.A.: 1993–94), G-2.0500.

9. Examples of theory in feminist psychotherapy include Ballou and Gabalac, 1985; Brown, 1994; Hare-Mustin and Maracek, 1990; Kaschak, 1992; Walters et al., 1988.

Numerous theorists rooted in family systems theory of psychotherapy are developing narrative therapy. Though this supporting discipline is not the primary focus of this project, examples of theory include Freedman and Combs, 1996; Monk, 1997; Parry and Doan, 1994; and White and Epston, 1990. Recent works in pastoral theology, which draw upon narrative theory more generally, include Capps, 1998; Gerkin, 1991; Lester, 1995, and Wimberly, 1991.

4. Equipping Caregivers

10. Stephen Ministries is a system of training in lay caring ministry. For information, contact Stephen Ministries, 8016 Dale, St. Louis, MO 63117-1449.

11. Fitchett's model discusses a process of gathering and interpreting information about seven key factors in a person's situation including the spiritual. Aspects of the spiritual dimension a caregiver listens for in Fitchett's model are similar to the Draper/Pruyser list of religious themes: (1) beliefs and meaning; (2) vocation and consequences of this sense of calling or duty; (3) experience and emotion, especially whether the person has had a "direct" religious experience; (4) courage and growth through times of change in one's faith; (5) rituals and practices as expression of meaning; (6) participation in a community of shared belief; (7) identifying who functions as an authority or guide for the person (Fitchett, 1993).

BIBLIOGRAPHY

Augsburger, D. W. *Pastoral Counseling Across Cultures.* Philadelphia: The Westminster Press, 1986.

Ballou, M. and N. Gabalac. *A Feminist Position on Mental Health,* Springfield, Ill.: Charles C. Thomas Publishers, 1985.

Bass, D. C. *Practicing Our Faith: A Way of Life for a Searching People.* San Francisco: Jossey-Bass, 1997.

Billman, K. D. "Pastoral Care as an Art of Community." In *The Arts of Ministry: Feminist-Womanist Approach,* edited by C. C. Neuger, 10–38. Louisville, Ky.: Westminster/John Knox, 1996.

Borsch, F. H. *Many Things in Parables: Extravagant Stories of New Community.* Philadelphia: Fortress Press, 1988.

Brammer, L. M. *The Helping Relationship: Process and Skills.* 4th ed. Englewood Cliffs, N.J.: Prentice Hall, 1988.

Brown, L. S. *Subversive Dialogue: Theory in Feminist Therapy.* New York: Basic Books, 1994.

Brueggemann, W. and G. W. Stroup, eds. *Many Voices, One God: Being Faithful in a Pluralistic World.* Louisville, Ky.: Westminster/John Knox Press, 1998.

Capps, D. *Biblical Approaches to Pastoral Counseling.* Philadelphia: Westminster Press, 1981.

———. *The Depleted Self: Sin in an Age of Narcissism.* Minneapolis: Fortress Press, 1993.

———. *Living Stories: Pastoral Counseling in Congregational Context.* Minneapolis: Augsburg Fortress, 1998.

———. *Pastoral Care and Hermeneutics.* Philadelphia: Fortress Press, 1984.

———. *Reframing: A New Method in Pastoral Counseling.* Minneapolis: Fortress Press, 1990.

Campbell, A. V. *Rediscovering Pastoral Care.* Philadelphia: Westminster Press, 1981.

Charry, D. *Mental Health Skills for Clergy.* Valley Forge, Pa.: Judson Press, 1981.

Chopp, R. *The Power to Speak: Feminism, Language, God.* New York: Crossroad, 1989.

———. *The Praxis of Suffering: An Interpretation of Liberation and Political Theologies.* Maryknoll, N.Y.: Orbis Books, 1989.

Chopp, R. S. and S. G. Davaney, eds. *Horizons in Feminist Theology: Identity, Tradition, and Norms.* Minneapolis: Fortress Press, 1997.

Clinebell, H. *Basic Types of Pastoral Care and Counseling.* Nashville: Abingdon, 1984.

————. *Understanding and Counseling the Person with Alcohol, Drug, and Behavioral Addictions.* Nashville: Abingdon Press, 1998.

Couture, P. *Blessed Are the Poor? Women's Poverty, Family Policy, and Practical Theology.* Nashville: Abingdon Press, 1991.

Couture, P. and R. Hunter, eds. *Pastoral Care and Social Conflict.* Nashville: Abingdon, 1995.

Coyle, S. "A Covenanting Process in Pastoral Home Visits." *The Journal of Pastoral Care.* 39 (1985): 96–109.

Doehring, C. Taking Care: *Monitoring Power Dynamics and Relational Boundaries in Pastoral Care and Counseling.* Nashville: Abingdon Press, 1995.

Draper, E. and G. Meyer, Z. Parzen, G. Samuelson. "On the Diagnostic Value of Religious Ideation." *Archives of General Psychiatry* 13 (Sept. 1965): 202–07.

Egan, G. *The Skilled Helper: A Problem Management Approach to Helping.* 5th ed. Pacific Grove, CA: Brooks/Cole Pub., 1994.

————. *Exercises in Helping Skills: A Manual to Accompany the Skilled Helper.* 5th ed. Pacific Grove, Calif.: Brooks/Cole Pub., 1994.

Faber, H. *Pastoral Care in the Modern Hospital.* London: SCM Press, 1971; Philadelphia: Westminster Press, 1971.

Faber, H. and E. van der Schoot. *The Art of Pastoral Conversation.* Nashville: Abingdon Press, 1965.

Fitchett, G. *Assessing Spiritual Needs: A Guide for Caregivers.* Minneapolis: Augsburg Press, 1993.

Fortune, M. *Is Nothing Sacred? When Sex Invades the Pastoral Relationship.* San Francisco: Harper, 1989.

Fortune, M. M. and J. N. Poling. *Sexual Abuse by Clergy: A Crisis for the Church.* Decatur, Ga.: Journal of Pastoral Care Publications, 1994.

Frank-Plumlee, K. V. "A Study of the Theology and Practice of Pastoral Visitation in the Christian Church (Disciples of Christ) in Kansas." D.Min., 1988. San Francisco Theological Seminary.

Freedman, J. and G. Combs. *Narrative Therapy.* New York: W. W. Norton, 1996.

Furniss, G. M. *The Social Context of Pastoral Care: Defining the Life Situation.* Louisville, Ky.: Westminster/John Knox Press, 1994.

Gerkin, C. *The Living Human Document: Revisioning Pastoral Counseling in a Hermeneutical Mode.* Nashville: Abingdon Press, 1984.

————. *Prophetic Pastoral Practice: A Christian Vision of Life Together.* Nashville: Abingdon Press, 1991.

Graham, L. K. *Care of Persons, Care of Worlds: A Psychosystems Approach to Pastoral Care and Counseling.* Nashville: Abingdon Press, 1992.

————. *Discovering Images of God: Narratives of Care Among Lesbians and Gays.* Louisville, Ky.: Westminster/John Knox Press, 1997.

Gunderson, G. *Deeply Woven Roots: Improving the Quality of Life in Your Community.* Minneapolis: Fortress Press, 1995.

Guthrie, S. C. *Christian Doctrine.* Rev. ed. Louisville, Ky.: Westminster/John Knox Press, 1994. An accessible discussion of theological issues from a Reformed perspective.

Hare-Mustin, R. and J. Marecek. *Making a Difference: Psychology and the Construction of Gender.* New Haven: Yale University Press, 1990.

Haugk, K. C. *Christian Caregiving: A Way of Life.* Minneapolis: Augsburg Publishing, 1984.

Hiltner, S. *The Christian Shepherd.* Nashville: Abingdon Press, 1959.

————. *Preface to Pastoral Theology.* Nashville: Abingdon Press, 1958.

Holifield, E. B. *A History of Pastoral Care in America: From Salvation to Self-Realization.* Nashville: Abingdon Press, 1983.

Hollies, L. H. *Womanistcare: How to Tend the Souls of Women.* Joliet, Ill.: Woman to Woman Ministries, Inc., 1991.

Houts, D. *Clergy Sexual Ethics: A Workshop Guide.* JPCP Monograph 3. Journal of Pastoral Care Publications, Inc., 1991.

Hoyt, T. "Testimony." In *Practicing Our Faith: A Way of Life for a Searching People,* edited by D. C. Bass, 91–103. San Francisco: Jossey-Bass Pub., 1997.

Hunter, R., ed. *Dictionary of Pastoral Care and Counseling.* Nashville: Abingdon Press, 1990.

Ivey, A. E., N. B. Gluckstern, and M. B. Ivey. *Basic Attending Skills.* 3rd ed. North Amherst, Mass.: Microtraining Associates, 1997.

Jackson, E. N. "Pastoral Calling and Visitation." In *Dictionary of Pastoral Care and Counseling,* edited by R. Hunter, 115–16. Nashville: Abingdon Press, 1990.

Kaschak, E. *Engendered Lives: A New Psychology of Women's Experience.* New York: Basic Books, 1992.

Krass, A. C. "Growing Together in Spirituality: Pastor and Parish Have a Check-Up." *Christian Century* 104 (1987): 311–14.

Lester, A. *Hope in Pastoral Care and Counseling.* Louisville, Ky.: Westminster/John Knox Press, 1995.

Lester, A. and J. Lester. *It Takes Two: The Joy of Intimate Marriage.* Louisville, Ky.: Westminster/John Knox Press, 1998.

Lewis, G. D. *Explorations in Ministry: A Report on the Ministry in the '70s Project.* New York: IDOC North America, 1971.

Liberman, A. and M. J. Woodruff. *Risk Management.* Minneapolis: Fortress Press, 1993.

Lyle, B. *Building Relationships Through Pastoral Visitation.* Valley Forge, Pa.: Judson Press, 1984.

McFague, S. *Metaphorical Theology: Models of God in Religious Language.* Philadelphia: Fortress Press, 1982.

Marshall, J. L. *Pastoral Counseling with Women in Lesbian Relationships.* Louisville, Ky.: Westminster/John Knox Press, 1997.

Migliore, D. L. *Faith Seeking Understanding: An Introduction to Christian Theology.* Grand Rapids, Mich.: Eerdmans Publishing Company, 1991.

Miles, R. *The Pastor as Moral Guide.* Minneapolis: Fortress Press, 1999.

Miller, W. R. and K. A. Jackson. *Practical Psychology for Pastors.* 2d ed. Englewood Cliffs, N.J.: Prentice-Hall, Inc., 1995.

Miller-McLemore, B. J. *Also a Mother: Work and Family as Theological Dilemma.* Nashville: Abingdon Press, 1994.

Mitchell, K. and H. Anderson. *All Our Losses, All Our Griefs: Resources for Pastoral Care.* Philadelphia: The Westminster Press, 1983.

Moessner, J. S., ed. *Through the Eyes of Women: Insights for Pastoral Care.* Minneapolis: Fortress Press, 1996.

Moltmann, J. *The Crucified God.* London: SCM Press, 1974.

Monk, G., et al. *Narrative Therapy in Practice: The Archaeology of Hope.* San Francisco: Jossey-Bass, 1997.

Neuger, C. C. "Pastoral Counseling as an Art of Personal Political Activism." In *The Arts of Ministry: Feminist-Womanist Approaches,* edited by C. C.Neuger, 88–117. Louisville, Ky.: Westminster/John Knox Press, 1996.

Neuger, C. C., ed. *The Arts of Ministry: Feminist-Womanist Approaches.* Louisville, Ky.: Westminster/John Knox Press, 1996.

Nichols, M. P. and R. C. Schwartz. *Family Therapy: Concepts and Methods.* 3rd ed. Boston: Allyn and Bacon, 1995.

Nouwen, H. *The Wounded Healer.* New York: Doubleday & Co., 1972.

Noyce, G. B. *The Art of Pastoral Conversation.* Atlanta: John Knox Press, 1981.

Oates, W. E. *The Christian Pastor.* 3rd ed. Philadelphia: The Westminster Press, 1982.

———. "Pastoral Visitation and/or Initiative." In *Explorations in Ministry: A Report on the Ministry in the '70s Project,* edited by G. D. Lewis, 165–73. New York: IDOC North America, 1971.

Oden, T. *Pastoral Theology: Essentials of Ministry.* San Francisco: Harper and Row,1983.

Oglesby, W. B. *Biblical Themes for Pastoral Care.* Nashville: Abingdon Press, 1980.

O'Hanlon, W. H. and M. Weiner-Davis. *In Search of Solutions: A New Direction in Psychotherapy.* New York: W. W. Norton, 1989.

Parry, A. and R. E. Doan. *Story Revisions: Narrative Therapy in the Postmodern World.* New York: Guilford Press, 1994.

Patton, J. *Pastoral Care in Context: An Introduction to Pastoral Care.* Louisville, Ky.: Westminster/John Knox Press, 1993.

Penner, C. and J. Penner. *The Gift of Sex: A Guide to Sexual Fulfillment.* Dallas: Word Pub., 1981.

Poling, J. *The Abuse of Power: A Theological Problem.* Nasvhille: Abingdon Press, 1991.

Poling, J. and C. Neuger. *The Care of Men.* Nashville: Abingdon Press, 1996.

Presbyterian Church, U.S.A. (PCUSA). *Book of Common Worship.* Prepared by the Theology and Worship Ministry Unit for the Presbyterian Church, U.S.A. and the Cumberland Presbyterian Church. Louisville, Ky.: Westminster/John Knox Press, 1993.

———. "Directory for Worship." *The Constitution of the Presbyterian Church (U.S.A.)* W-6.1003. Louisville, Ky.: Office of the General Assembly, 1998.

———. "Growing in the Life of Christian Faith." Report commended by the 201st General Assembly. Louisville, Ky.: Distribution Management Services, PCUSA, 1989.

———.*Services for Occasions of Pastoral Care: The Worship of God.* Prepared by The Ministry Unit on Theology and Worship, PCUSA. Louisville, Ky.: Westminster/John Knox Press, 1990.

Pruyser, P. *The Minister as Diagnostician.* Philadelphia: The Westminster Press, 1976.

Ramsey, N. *Pastoral Diagnosis: A Resource for Ministries of Care and Counseling.* Minneapolis: Fortress Press, 1998.

Ramshaw, E. *Ritual and Pastoral Care.* Philadelphia: Fortress Press, 1987.

Rando, T. A. *Grief, Dying, and Death: Clinical Interventions for Caregivers.* Champaign, Ill.: Research Press Co., 1984.

Rassieur, C. "Career Burnout Prevention Among Pastoral Counselors and Pastors." In *Handbook for Basic Types of Pastoral Care and Counseling,* edited by Stone and Clements, 256–72. Nashville: Abingdon Press, 1991.

Robb, N. "Worship Life: Pastoral Care as Witness." *Contact* III (1993): 3–9.

Rogers, C. R. *Client-Centered Therapy: Its Current Practice, Implications, and Theory.* Boston: Houghton Mifflin, 1951.

———. *On Becoming a Person: A Therapist's View of Psychotherapy.* Boston: Houghton Mifflin, 1961.

Russell, L. *The Future of Partnership.* Philadelphia: Westminster/John Knox Press, 1979.

———. *Growth in Partnership.* Philadelphia: Westminster/John Knox Press, 1981.

———. *Household of Freedom.* Philadelphia: Westminster/John Knox Press, 1987.

Shores, T. L. "A Course in Pastoral Visitation for Student Pastors of the Dalton District." D. Min., 1987. Candler School of Theology, Emory University.

Stone, H. *Brief Pastoral Counseling: Short-term Approaches and Strategies.* Minneapolis: Fortress Press, 1994.

———. *The Caring Church: A Guide for Lay Pastoral Care.* Minneapolis: Fortress Press, 1991.

———. *Crisis Counseling.* Rev. ed. Minneapolis: Fortress Press, 1993.

———. *Depression and Hope: New Insights for Pastoral Counseling.* Minneapolis: Fortress Press, 1998.

Stone, H. and J. Duke. *How to Think Theologically.* Minneapolis: Fortress Press, 1996.

Stone, H. and W. Clements. *Handbook for Basic Types of Pastoral Care and Counseling.* Nashville: Abingdon Press, 1991.

Switzer, D. *Pastoral Care Emergencies: Ministering to People in Crisis.* New York: Paulist Press, 1989.

Taylor, C. *The Skilled Pastor: Counseling as the Practice of Theology.* Minneapolis: Fortress Press, 1991.

United Presbyterian Church, U.S.A. "Biblical Authority and Interpretation." A Resource Document Received by the 194th General Assembly (1982) of the United Presbyterian Church, U.S.A. Louisville, Ky.: Office of the General Assembly, 1982.

van Beek, A. M. *Cross-Cultural Counseling.* Minneapolis: Fortress Press, 1998.

Walter, J. L. and J. Peller. *Becoming Solution-Focused in Brief Therapy.* New York: Brunner/Mazel, 1992.

Walters, M. et al. *The Invisible Web: Gender Patterns in Family Relationships.* New York: Guilford Press, 1988.

White, M. and D. Epston. *Narrative Means to Therapeutic Ends.* New York: W. W. Norton, 1990.

Wicks, R. J., R. D. Parsons, and D. Capps. *Clinical Handbook of Pastoral Counseling.* 2 vols. New York: Paulist Press, 1993.

Wimberly, E. P. *African American Pastoral Care.* Nashville: Abingdon Press, 1991.

Woodruff, C. R. "Pastoral Conversation." In *Dictionary of Pastoral Care and Counseling,* edited by R. Hunter, 227–28. Nashville: Abingdon Press, 1990.